Cuddly
Crochet Critters

26 Animal Patterns

Megan Kreiner

DOVER PUBLICATIONS, INC.
Mineola, New York

Cover and animal pattern photography: Brian Kraus

General assembly and all pattern illustrations: Megan Kreiner

Step-by-step photography (pp. 3 to 10): Pat Olski, crocheter;
Charles Young, photographer

The publisher would like to thank the Kreiner kids
for providing us with the names of the cuddly crochet critters
we've gotten to know so well.

Copyright

Copyright © 2019 by Megan Kreiner
All rights reserved.

Bibliographical Note

Cuddly Crochet Critters: 26 Animal Patterns is a new work, first published by
Dover Publications, Inc., in 2019. The author is represented by MacGregor Literary, Inc.

Library of Congress Cataloging-in-Publication Data

Names: Kreiner, Megan, 1981– author.
Title: Cuddly crochet critters: 26 animal patterns / Megan Kreiner.
Description: Mineola, N.Y.: Dover Publications, Inc., 2019.
Identifiers: LCCN 2019005488| ISBN 9780486833958 | ISBN 048683395X
Subjects: LCSH: Crocheting— Patterns. | Soft toy making—Patterns. | Stuffed animals
   (Toys)
Classification: LCC TT829 .K744 2019 | DDC 746.43/4041—dc23 LC record available at
https://lccn.loc.gov/2019005488

Manufactured in the United States by LSC Communications
83395X01   2019
www.doverpublications.com

Contents

Patterns

Dedication

For Lydia

Introduction

Get ready for some extra-chunky fun with this collection of oversized cuddly crochet critters! These projects whip up quickly into soft and pillowy pals that are perfect for naps and travel and are easily customizable. Starting with a basic body shape, each pattern includes a variety of unique add-ons such as snouts, muzzles, horns, ears, and tails that can be mixed and matched to create any kind of critter you can imagine! Turn a whale into a narwhal by adding a unicorn's horn or turn a duck into a platypus by adding a beaver's feet and tail. The possibilities are endless!

I hope you'll take the opportunity to experiment with these patterns and make a custom crochet critter that's as unique as you are!

Happy Crocheting!

—Megan Kreiner of MK Crochet

Getting Started

Yarn, hook, needles, and stitch markers

Materials

Before you begin on your first critter, check over your materials to make sure you have everything you need to complete your project!

Yarns: To make your chunky critters super-sized, it's recommended you use Super Bulky Bernat® Blanket™ Yarn (100% polyester). It comes in 10.5oz/300g skeins and in a wide range of colors. You should expect to use between 200 and 250 grams or 150 to 170 yards for each project.

In addition to this super-bulky yarn, you will also need 2–3 yards of chunky black yarn for smaller details such as eyebrows. For the samples in this book, I've used Bulky Berroco® Comfort® Chunky Yarn (50% super fine acrylic, 50% super fine nylon).

TIP: The blanket yarn used for these projects can sometimes snap when pulled too hard, so take care when pulling on the yarn when closing the holes in the middle of your adjustable rings.

Safety Eyes & Noses: The extra-large eyes and noses featured in this book were all purchased online through the website www.glasseyesonline.com. It is important to note that pillows intended for children under 3 should utilize alternative eyes and noses (page 13) as plastic safety eyes and noses can pose a choking hazard.

Plastic safety eyes and noses

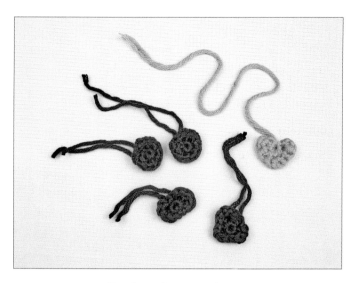

Crocheted eyes and noses

Stuffing: Polyester fiberfill stuffing is readily available at most craft stores and will maintain its shape over time. Each pillow critter takes about one 12-ounce bag of stuffing to complete.

Notions & Tools

A short list of tools will help make the process of putting together your chunky critters quick and easy:

Hooks: For super-bulky yarn, you will be using a size M/N (9.0mm) hook. There are lots of options in regard to materials and handle styles for crochet hooks. To find the one that works best for you, try to hold the hooks in your hand before you make your purchase to ensure a comfortable fit.

Because you are making pillow critters and not garments, your stitch gauge and overall sizing is not crucial. However, if you find that your stitches aren't tight enough and your stuffing shows through, try reducing your hook size.

Scissors: Fabric scissors used exclusively for yarn will help ensure clean cuts and quick snips.

Tapestry Needles: You will need a large steel tapestry needle with an eye large enough to accommodate extra-chunky yarns. Avoid plastic tapestry needles since they can sometimes bend and break when going through multiple layers of crochet and stuffing.

Stitch Counter: A counter can help you keep track of where you are in your pattern.

Large Safety Pins: Use safety pins when a pattern calls out for "place markers" (pm) to help mark useful landmarks on your work. Smaller place markers such as split rings can sometimes slip off or get lost among the large stitches.

Marking Pins: For projects using bulky yarn, you might find that regular straight pins are not large enough to hold anything in place. Look for larger bamboo straight pins to help keep your project pieces together while you sew!

Project Bags: A small project bag (such as a canvas pencil case) is great for storing smaller tools and notions while a larger canvas shopping bag can hold everything else needed for your current project.

Resources

Yarnspirations
www.yarnspirations.com
Bernat Yarn

Berroco
www.berroco.com
Berroco Yarn

Glass Eyes online
www.glasseyesonline.com
Online shop featuring a wide variety of safety eyes and noses

Hobbs Bonded Fibers
www.hobbsbondedfibers.com
Poly-down fiberfill toy stuffing and black batting, available at local craft stores

Clover
www.clover-usa.com
Hooks and notions, available at local craft stores

Fiskars
www.fiskars.com
Scissors and cutting mats, available at local craft stores

Crochet Stitches & Techniques

The projects in this book are considered "Easy" (a step above the novice/beginner level) and require a few basic crochet stitches to complete. If you are new to crocheting, this section will provide an overview of all the stitches used for the patterns in this book.

To make the details easier to see, we'll be using a thinner yarn for our stitch-making examples.

Slipknot

1. Make a loop with a 6" tail. Overlap the loop on top of the working yarn coming out of the skein.

2. Slip your hook into the loop and under the working yarn and gently pull to tighten the yarn around the hook.

Yarn Over (YO)

Wrap the yarn over your hook from back to front.

Chain (ch)

1. Make a slipknot on your hook.

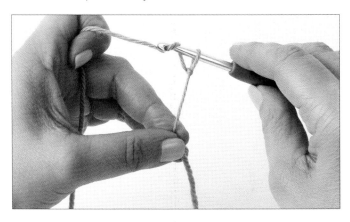

2. Yarn over (YO) and draw the yarn through the loop on your hook. You should now have one loop on your hook with a slipknot below it.

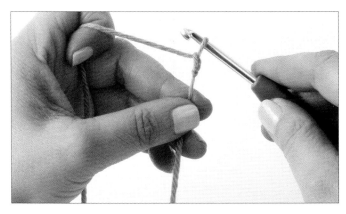

3. Repeat Step 2 until you've reached the specified number of chain stitches. When counting, only the chains below the loop on the hook should be counted.

Slip Stitch (sl st)

1. Insert your hook into the next chain or stitch.

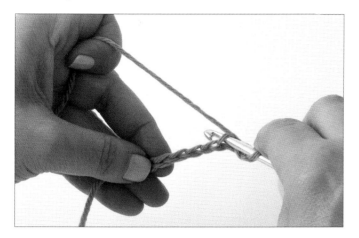

2. While keeping your tension as loose as possible, YO and draw the yarn through the stitch and the loop on your hook.

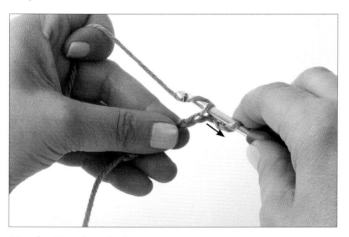

Single Crochet (sc)

1. Insert your hook into a chain or stitch and YO. Draw the yarn through the chain or stitch. You will have 2 loops on your hook.

2. YO and draw yarn through both loops on your hook to complete the single crochet.

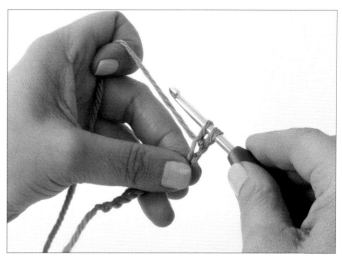

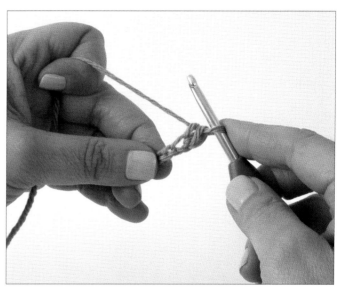

Half Double Crochet (hdc)

1. YO and insert your hook into a chain or stitch. YO a second time and draw the yarn through the chain or stitch. You will have 3 loops on your hook.

2. YO and draw yarn through all three loops on your hook to complete the half double crochet.

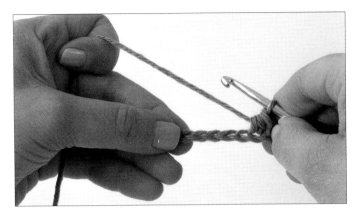

Increases (Sc 2 in next st)

Work 2 or more stitches into the same stitch when indicated.

Decreases

There are two kinds of decreases used in this book's patterns: Single Crochet Decreases and Skipped Stitches.

Single Crochet 2 together (Sc2tog)

1. Insert your hook into the next stitch, YO and draw the yarn through the stitch. You will have 2 loops on your hook.

2. Repeat Step 1 in following stitch. You will have 3 loops on your hook.

3. YO and draw yarn through all three loops on your hook to finish the decrease.

Skip (sk)

Per the pattern instructions, count and skip the number of stitches indicated before working the next stitch in the pattern.

Working in back loops (bl), front loops (fl) and both loops (tbl)

For all patterns, work in both loops of a stitch except when the pattern instructs that a stitch should be worked in the back loop or front loop. The front loop is the loop closest to you. The back loop is behind the front loop. If a round or row begins with "In bl" or "In fl" work entire rnd/row in that manner unless you are instructed to switch.

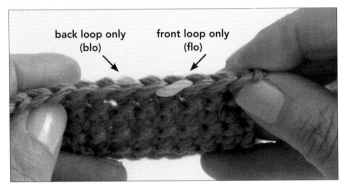

back loop only (blo)   front loop only (flo)

Working in the round

Many patterns in this book are worked in a spiral round in which there is no slip stitch or chains between rounds. You just keep right on crocheting from one round to the next. If needed, use a stitch marker to help keep track of where your rounds begin and end.

Adjustable Ring (AR)

The adjustable ring is a great technique that will minimize the hole that commonly appears in the middle of a starting round.

1. Form a ring with your yarn, leaving a 6" tail. Insert the hook into the loop as if you were making a slip-knot.

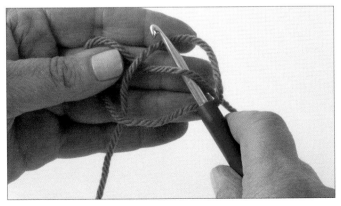

2. YO the hook and pull through the loop to make a slip stitch but do not tighten the loop.

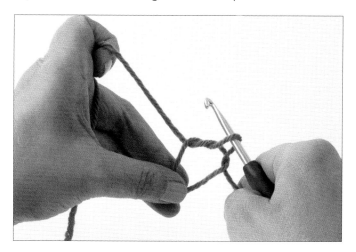

3. Ch 1 and then sc over both strands of yarn that make up the edge of the adjustable ring until you've reached the number of stitches indicated in the pattern. To close the center of the ring, pull firmly on the yarn tail.

To start your next round, work your next stitch in the first single crochet of the completed adjustable ring. If the pattern requires a semicircle shape (like for an ear), ch 1 and turn the work so that the back of the piece faces you before working the next row in your pattern.

Working around a chain

When working around a chain of stitches, you'll first work in the back ridge loops of the chain and then in the front loops of the chain to create your first round.

1. Make a chain per the pattern instructions. To begin round 1, work your first stitch in the back ridge loop of the second chain from your hook (feel free to mark this stitch with a stitch marker to make it easy to find). Work the rest of your stitches into the back ridge loops of the chain until you've reached the last chain above the slipknot. Work the indicated number of stitches into the back ridge loop of this last chain.

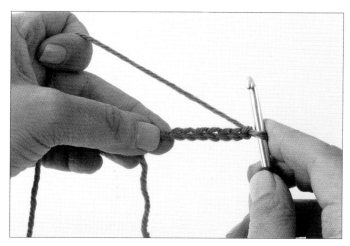

2. When you're ready to work the other side of the chain, rotate your work so the front loops of the chain face up. Starting in the next chain, insert your hook under the two front loops of the chain to work your next stitch.

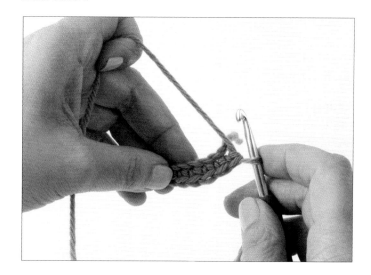

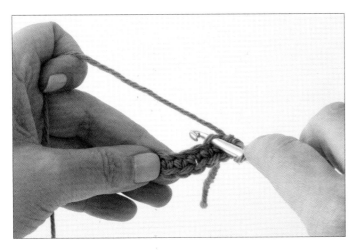

3. Once you have finished working the rest of the stitches into the front loops of round 1, continue on to round 2 (indicated by your stitch marker).

Right Side (RS) & Wrong Side (WS)

When working in the round, the side of your pattern perceived as the "right side" will affect which part of the stitch is the back loop versus the front loop. As a general rule, the 6" tail left over from forming the adjustable ring will usually lie on the wrong side (WS) of the piece. The same can be said for patterns that begin by working around a chain provided you hold the 6" yarn tail at the back of your work as you crochet the first round.

Changing Colors

Work the stitch prior to the color change right up to the last step in which you would normally draw the yarn through the loop(s) on your hook to complete the stitch.

To change colors, YO the hook with your new color and draw the new color through the remaining loop(s) on your hook, completing the stitch. You can then continue on to the next stitch in the new color.

Jogless Color Changes

When working color changes in the round, the colors will sometimes appear to "break" or "jog" into a step-like pattern from one round to the next. This can be undesirable for patterns with stripes (like the tiger). To help reduce the color jog, and to blend the beginning and end of your color changes, complete the last stitch of your round in the first color and then slip stitch in the front loop of the first stitch of the next round and pull firmly.

Working in the back loop of the same stitch, drop your first color and slip stitch with your new color. Pull yarn firmly, ch 1, and pull yarn firmly again.

Working in the next stitch, complete your first stitch as written. Place a marker if desired to help mark where your round begins. You will skip over the slip stitches and ch 1 when you are ready to begin the next round.

Please note that this technique will offset your round's first stitch.

Working in Surface Stitches

You can add details such as a lion's mane by crocheting directly onto the surface of your work.

To join your yarn to the surface of your work, select a starting location and insert your hook through a stitch loop on the surface of your work.

YO the hook with your working yarn and draw the hook back through the surface stitch to pull up a loop. Ch 1.

Work your first stitch in the same surface loop to begin your pattern (so, if your pattern begins with a single crochet stitch, you will work one single crochet stitch into your surface loop).

Continue to crochet your pattern into the surface loops of your work as written.

Assembly & Embroidery Stitches

Assemble and add finishing touches to your creations with a few simple sewing and embroidery stitches.

Whipstitch

Use this stitch to close seams and attach open edges on your work. Using your tapestry needle and yarn, draw your needle and yarn through your work and catch the edge(s) of the second piece you wish to sew in place. Pull the yarn through the edge(s) before drawing the yarn through your work again in a spiral-like motion. Continue until the seam is closed or the piece is attached.

Short & Long Stitches

Shape the surface of your character with short and long stitches. With your yarn and a metal tapestry needle, draw the yarn up through the surface of your piece (A) and then reinsert the needle in a different location (B). Repeat if desired to double or triple up the yarn. To cinch the surface of your piece, pull the yarn firmly as you work.

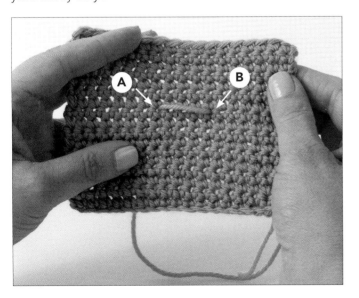

Mattress Stitch

The mattress stitch will give you a nice tight seam between various toy pieces, such as for sewing down the open edges of tails and muzzles and for sewing crochet surfaces together like heads to bodies.

Select a point on the surface or edge of your first piece and insert the needle from A to B and pull the yarn through. Cross over to the surface of your second piece and draw your needle in and out from C to D with the entry point at C lining up between points A and B on the first surface. Return to the first surface and insert your needle directly next to exit point B. Continue to work back and forth in this manner until seam is closed, pulling firmly after every few stitches to ensure a clean, tight seam.

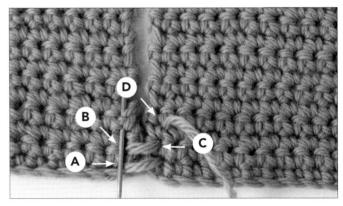

TIP: Leave long yarn tails when you fasten off your arms and legs. When assembling, use straight pins to attach all your limbs to the body to ensure everything is even and balanced. Then, using the leftover yarn tails, place a single stitch at each straight pin to tack your pieces in place. Remove the pins and finish sewing your pieces down using a whipstitch or mattress stitch.

Satin Stitch

Apply satin stitches by grouping short- or medium-length stitches closely together to build up a shape or fill an area with color. This can be a great option for adding spots or baby-safe eyes to your critter.

Running Stitch

Draw your yarn in and out of the surface of your piece in a dashed-line pattern.

Backstitch

Use this stitch to create solid line details on the surface of your work. (A) Begin by drawing the yarn up through the surface of your piece. (B) Reinsert the needle to the right, (C) then bring it up slightly to the left of the first stitch as shown. Continue to work in this manner to make a solid line of stitches.

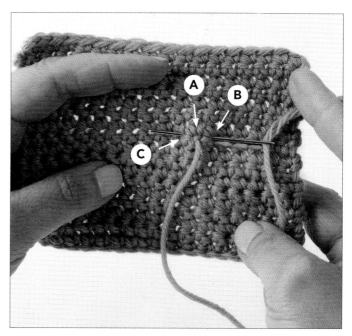

General Assembly Tips

All the patterns in this book are assembled using the same basic techniques. This section will give you a general illustrated overview of how to piece your cuddly critter together. For a review of the stitches used to assembly your project, please refer to Assembly & Embroidery Stitches on page 9.

TIP: Because projects crocheted using blanket yarn feature large, chunky stitches, using regular straight pins to hold your pieces together for assembly might prove challenging. Instead, try using larger bamboo straight pins to position your pattern pieces together before sewing your seams.

It is recommended that you partially stuff the front half of your critter before installing the eyes so you can get a better feel for the shape of the body and face. If using plastic safety eyes, install the backings to secure the eyes. For critters intended for children under 3, sew on crocheted eyes (page 13) or embroider a tight grouping of satin stitches (page 10) for eyes onto the front of the face.

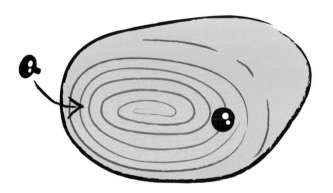

Once your eyes are installed, add more stuffing to the body if needed before sewing the edges of the back opening closed using a mattress stitch.

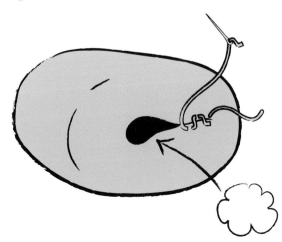

If you would like to add cheek shaping to your critter's face, loop a long stitch of yarn out from the middle of the ch-8 in the center of the face and into the bottom of the head (around Rnd 6) before drawing the yarn out through the starting point in the center of the face again. Repeat 2–3 times, pulling tightly to shape the cheeks.

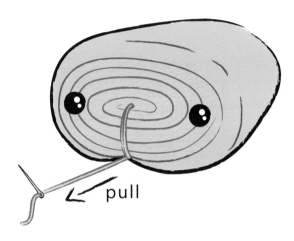

pull

If your pattern includes a muzzle that requires a nose, install the nose before sewing the muzzle to the front of the face. If a plastic safety nose is not available, or if you need a safe alternative for children under 3, refer to the crocheted nose patterns on page 13 or embroider a tight grouping of satin stitches (page 10) for a nose.

Sew the edge of your muzzle to the front of your critter's face using a mattress stitch, stuffing the muzzle before closing up the seam.

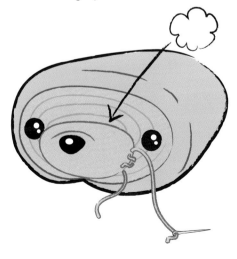

If adding a lip cleft below a plastic safety nose, tie the middle of an 18–20" strand of bulky black yarn around the post of the nose. Thread your tapestry needle with the yarn tails, draw a long stitch down over the front of the muzzle, and fasten off beneath the muzzle to create the lip cleft detail. The same long stitch can also be embroidered onto the muzzle when using child-safe crocheted noses (page 13).

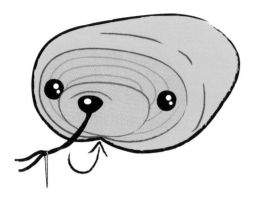

If your pattern includes a belly patch, position the belly patch in the desired location. It is recommended that you pin down the edges to ensure even placement and a smooth fit. Sew the edge down using a backstitch.

The same pin and backstitch technique can also be used when installing spots.

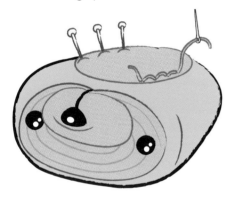

For ears small or large, use a whipstitch to attach the base of the ear to the head. Wings and fringes can also be attached using a whipstitch.

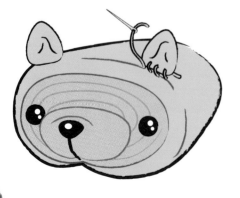

For horns and tails, stuff your pattern piece, pin your work into place, and sew open edge down using a mattress stitch.

Install a belly patch first before sewing legs to the body. Mattress stitch the open edge of the legs to the bottom of the body but leave the yarn tails unsecured until all legs are sewn in place to allow for easier removal and adjustments. Once you are satisfied with the leg placement, fasten off the yarn tails and weave in the ends.

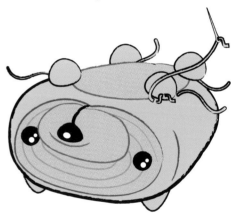

Double up an 18–20" strand of bulky black yarn on a tapestry needle to add embroidered details such as eyebrows, gills, whiskers, or lip clefts for those perfect finishing touches.

If you want eyebrows to have a bit of a curve, embroider a loose long stitch over the top of each eye. Shape the eyebrow stitch into an arch by adding a small stitch over the long stitch to hold the eyebrow in place.

Crocheted Eyes & Noses

To avoid a potential choking hazard, plastic safety eyes and noses should not be given to children under 3. Use these instructions for sew-on eyes and noses that you can use on all projects to keep your creations safe for kids of all ages!

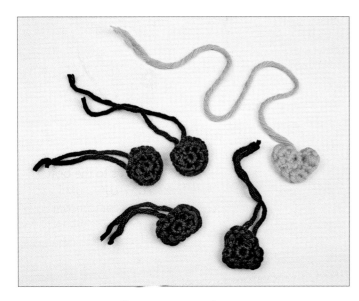

Sew-on eyes and noses

Yarn

Worsted Berroco® Comfort® in **(A)** #9734 Liquorice and **(B)** #9723 Rosebud

Notions

- Size G (4.0mm) or H (5.0mm) crochet hook
- Large steel tapestry needle
- Scissors

Eyes

With A, make a 6-st AR.

Rnd 1: Sc 2 in each st around—12 sts.

Rnd 2: In bl, sc 12.

Rnd 3: Sc2tog 6 times.

Fasten off yarn, leaving a long tail for sewing.

Triangle Nose

With A, make a 6-st AR.

Rnd 1: Sc 2 in next st, (sc 1, hdc 1, ch 1, sc 1) in next st, sl st 1, (sc 1, ch 1, sc 1) in next st, sl st 1, (sc 1, hdc 1, ch 1, sc 1) in next st.

Fasten off, leaving a long tail for sewing.

Heart Nose

With B, make a 5-st AR but do not join. Turn and work semicircle shape in rows.

Row 1: Ch 1, (sc 1, hdc 1, sc 1) next st, sc 1, (sc 1, ch 1, sc 1) in next st, sc 1, (sc 1, hdc 1, sc 1) next st.

Cut yarn and pull through current stitch to fasten off, leaving a long tail for sewing.

Oval Nose

With A, make an 8-st AR.

Rnd 1: Sl st 1, hdc 2 in next 2 sts, sl st 2, hdc 2 in next 2 sts, sl st 1.

Fasten off, leaving a long tail for sewing.

Want to make some mini versions of your cuddly critters? You can downsize the patterns using the following suggested yarn and hook combinations.

Chunky (Bulky): H (5.0mm) or I (5.5mm)

Worsted Weight (Medium): F (3.75mm) or G (4.0mm)

DK Weight/Light Worsted (Light): D (3.25mm) or E (3.5mm)

Sport/Baby (Fine): B (2.25mm) or C (2.75mm)

When experimenting with different yarns, aim to use the smallest hook size possible to ensure a tight stitch that won't let the stuffing show through; and don't forget to adjust the sizes of your safety eyes and noses accordingly if you wish to use them!

Penny Pig

Perfectly plump Penny Pig is a pink bundle
of adorable from snout to tail.

YARNS

Super Bulky Bernat® Blanket™ Yarn—
(A) #04758 Shell Pink (200yds/185m)

Bulky Berroco® Comfort®
Chunky—#5734 Liquorice (2yds/2m)

Optional (for child-safe eyes):
Worsted Berroco® Comfort®—#9734
Liquorice. See page 13 for pattern.

NOTIONS

- Size M/N (9.0mm) crochet hook
- Two 21mm black safety eyes
- Large steel tapestry needle
- Scissors
- Polyester fiberfill (12oz/340g)
- *Optional*: Large safety pins for place markers, bamboo straight pins

FINISHED SIZE

13" long, 9" wide, 7" tall

Penny Pig

Body

With A, loosely ch 8.

Rnd 1: Working in back ridge loops, sc 6, sc 3 in next st. Rotate chain so front loops of chain are facing up. Starting in next st, sc 5, sc 2 in next st—16 sts.

Rnd 2: Sc 2 in next st, sc 5, sc 2 in next 3 sts, sc 5, sc 2 in next 2 sts—22 sts.

Rnd 3: Sc 2 in next st, sc 7, sc 2 in next 4 sts, sc 7, sc 2 in next 3 sts—30 sts.

Rnd 4: Sc 2 in next 2 sts, sc 9, sc 2 in next 6 sts, sc 9, sc 2 in next 4 sts—42 sts.

Rnd 5: (Sc 3, sc 2 in next st, sc 3) 6 times—48 sts.

Rnd 6: (Sc 2, sc 2 in next st) 16 times—64 sts.

Rnds 7–8: Sc 64.

Rnd 9: (Sc 2, sc2tog) 16 times—48 sts.

Rnds 10–27: Sc 48.

Rnd 28: (Sc 2, sc2tog, sc 2) 8 times—40 sts.

Rnd 29: (Sc 3, sc2tog) 8 times—32 sts.

Rnd 30: (Sc 1, sc2tog, sc 1) 8 times—24 sts.

Rnd 31: (Sc 1, sc2tog) 8 times—16 sts.

Fasten off, leaving a long tail for sewing. Stuff body firmly, but do not close hole.

If using plastic safety eyes, attach eyes to the front of the body between Rnds 3 and 4. You may wish to remove a bit of stuffing after positioning the eyes to make installing the eye backings easier. For children under 3, sew on crocheted eyes (page 13) or embroider eyes using the bulky black yarn and a tight grouping of satin stitches (page 10).

Using a mattress stitch, bring the edges of the hole in the back of the body together and sew the seam closed in a straight line level with the ch-8 at the beginning of your work.

With A, draw a long stitch out from the middle of the ch-8 in the center of the face and into the bottom of the head (around Rnd 6) before drawing the yarn out through the starting point in the center of the face again. Repeat 2–3 times, pulling tightly to shape the cheeks.

Ears (make 2)

With A, loosely ch 4.

Row 1: Starting in 2nd ch from hook, sc 3 and turn—3 sts.

Row 2: Ch 1, sc 1, sk 1, sc 1 and turn—2 sts.

Row 3: Ch 1, sc2tog and pm—1 st.

Continue to sc evenly along the side, bottom edge, and opposite side of the ear until you reach the marker. (Sc 1, ch 2, sl st 1) in marked st, fasten off in next st and cut yarn, leaving a long tail for sewing.

Whipstitch the rounded base of the ears to the head about 4–5 rnds behind the eyes.

Curly Tail

With A, loosely ch 8.

Starting in 2nd ch from hook and working in back ridge loops, sc 2 in each st to end.

Fasten off, leaving a long tail for sewing. Attach tail to back of body.

Legs & Snout (make 5)

With A, make a 6-st AR.

Rnd 1: Sc 2 in each st around—12 sts.

Rnd 2: In bl, sc2tog 6 times—6 sts.

Fasten off, leaving a long tail for sewing.

Stuff and mattress stitch the open edge of the snout to the middle of the face and the legs to the bottom of the body (around Rnds 12–13 for the front legs and Rnds 22–23 for the back legs) with about 8 sts of space between the inside edges of the legs.

NOTE: When sewing the legs to the bottom of the body, leave the yarn tails unsecured until all 4 legs are sewn in place to allow for easier removal and adjustments. Once you are satisfied with the leg placement, fasten off the yarn tails and weave in the ends.

FINISHING: Double a long piece of the bulky black yarn on a tapestry needle and embroider 2 short stitches to the front of the snout for nostrils and an eyebrow over each eye.

Weave in any remaining yarn tails.

Davy Duck

A happy quacker with ruffled wings and floppy webbed feet,
Davy Duck is always ready to make a big splash!

YARNS

Super Bulky Bernat® Blanket™ Yarn—
(A) #12003 School Bus Yellow
(200yds/185m)
(B) #12002 Carrot Orange (50yds/45m)

Bulky Berroco® Comfort®
Chunky—#5734 Liquorice (2yds/2m)

Optional (for child-safe eyes):
Worsted Berroco® Comfort®—#9734
Liquorice. See page 13 for pattern.

NOTIONS

• Size M/N (9.0mm) crochet hook
• Two 21mm black safety eyes
• Large steel tapestry needle
• Scissors
• Polyester fiberfill (12oz/340g)
• *Optional:* Large safety pins for place markers, bamboo straight pins

FINISHED SIZE

13" long, 9" wide, 7" tall

Davy Duck

Body

With A, loosely ch 8.

Rnd 1: Working in back ridge loops, sc 6, sc 3 in next st. Rotate chain so front loops of chain are facing up. Starting in next st, sc 5, sc 2 in next st—16 sts.

Rnd 2: Sc 2 in next st, sc 5, sc 2 in next 3 sts, sc 5, sc 2 in next 2 sts—22 sts.

Rnd 3: Sc 2 in next st, sc 7, sc 2 in next 4 sts, sc 7, sc 2 in next 3 sts—30 sts.

Rnd 4: Sc 2 in next 2 sts, sc 9, sc 2 in next 6 sts, sc 9, sc 2 in next 4 sts—42 sts.

Rnd 5: (Sc 3, sc 2 in next st, sc 3) 6 times—48 sts.

Rnd 6: (Sc 2, sc 2 in next st) 16 times—64 sts.

Rnds 7–8: Sc 64.

Rnd 9: (Sc 2, sc2tog) 16 times—48 sts.

Rnds 10–27: Sc 48.

Rnd 28: (Sc 2, sc2tog, sc 2) 8 times—40 sts.

Rnd 29: (Sc 3, sc2tog) 8 times—32 sts.

Rnd 30: (Sc 1, sc2tog, sc 1) 8 times—24 sts.

Rnd 31: (Sc 1, sc2tog) 8 times—16 sts.

Fasten off, leaving a long tail for sewing. Stuff body firmly, but do not close hole.

If using plastic safety eyes, attach eyes to the front of the body between Rnds 3 and 4. You may wish to remove a bit of stuffing after positioning the eyes to make installing the eye backings easier. For children under 3, sew on crocheted eyes (page 13) or embroider eyes using the bulky black yarn and a tight grouping of satin stitches (page 10).

Using a mattress stitch, bring the edges of the hole in the back of the body together and sew the seam closed in a straight line level with the ch-8 at the beginning of your work.

With A, draw a long stitch out from the middle of the ch-8 in the center of the face and into the bottom of the head (around Rnd 6) before drawing the yarn out through the starting point in the center of the face again. Repeat 2–3 times, pulling tightly to shape the cheeks.

Duckbill

With B, loosely ch 11.

Rnd 1: Working in back ridge loops, sc 9, sc 3 in next st. Rotate chain so front loops of chain are facing up. Starting in next st, sc 8, sc 2 in next st—22 sts.

Rnd 2: Sc 22.

Fasten off, leaving a long tail for sewing. Stuff lightly, flatten seam, and sew shut. With B, whipstitch the back edge of the duckbill to the middle of the face slightly below the eyes.

Wings and Tail (make 3)

With A, make an 8-st AR, but do not join. Turn and work semicircle shape in rows.

Row 1: Ch 1, sl st 2, sc 2 in next 4 sts, sl st 2 and turn—12 sts.

Row 2: Ch 1, sl st 2, (sl st 1, ch 2, sl st 1) in next 8 sts, sl st 2.

Fasten off, leaving a long tail for sewing.

Sew straight edges of the wings to sides of body so the ruffled edges stick out.

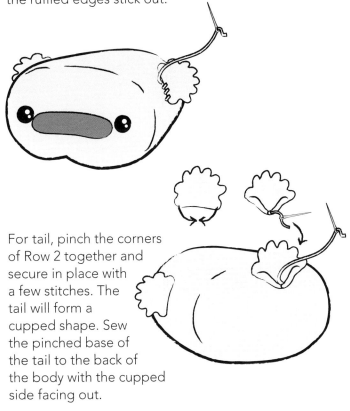

For tail, pinch the corners of Row 2 together and secure in place with a few stitches. The tail will form a cupped shape. Sew the pinched base of the tail to the back of the body with the cupped side facing out.

Feet (make 2)

With B, make a 7-st AR.

Rnd 1: Sl st 2, (sl st 1, ch 3, sl st 1) in next 3 sts, sl st 2.

Fasten off, leaving a long tail for sewing.

With the toes pointing toward the front of the body, mattress stitch the tops of the feet to the bottom of the body (around Rnds 22–23) with about 8 sts of space between the inside edges.

FINISHING: Double a long piece of the bulky black yarn on a tapestry needle and embroider an eyebrow over each eye.

Weave in any remaining yarn tails.

Shelly Sheep

Soft and lovable Shelly Sheep is always sleepy. And, if you make her a flock of friends, you'll have something to count before bedtime!

YARNS

Super Bulky Bernat® Blanket™ Yarn—
(A) #04005 White (180yds/165m)
(B) #04008 Vanilla (30yds/27m)
(C) #10040 Coal (20yds/18m)

Bulky Berroco® Comfort®
Chunky—#5734 Liquorice (2yds/2m)

Optional (for child-safe eyes):
Worsted Berroco® Comfort®—#9734
Liquorice. See page 13 for pattern.

NOTIONS

- Size M/N (9.0mm) crochet hook
- Two 21mm black safety eyes
- Large steel tapestry needle
- Scissors
- Polyester fiberfill (12oz/340g)
- *Optional*: Large safety pins for place markers, bamboo straight pins

FINISHED SIZE

13" long, 9" wide, 7" tall

Shelly Sheep

Body

Starting with B, loosely ch 8.

Rnd 1: Working in back ridge loops, sc 6, sc 3 in next st. Rotate chain so front loops of chain are facing up. Starting in next st, sc 5, sc 2 in next st—16 sts.

Rnd 2: Sc 2 in next st, sc 5, sc 2 in next 3 sts, sc 5, sc 2 in next 2 sts—22 sts.

Rnd 3: Sc 2 in next st, sc 7, sc 2 in next 4 sts, sc 7, sc 2 in next 3 sts—30 sts.

Rnd 4: Sc 2 in next 2 sts, sc 9, sc 2 in next 6 sts, sc 9, sc 2 in next 4 sts—42 sts.

Rnd 5: (Sc 3, sc 2 in next st, sc 3) 6 times—48 sts.

Rnd 6: (Sc 2, sc 2 in next st) 16 times—64 sts.

Cut B, change to A.

Rnd 7: In fl, (sc 1, ch 2, sc 1) 32 times to create woolly ruffle.

Rnd 8: Working directly behind the base of the woolly ruffle in the bls of Rnd 6, sc 64—64 sts.

Rnd 9: Sc 64.

Rnd 10: (Sc 2, sc2tog) 16 times—48 sts.

Rnds 11–28: Sc 48.

Rnd 29: (Sc 2, sc2tog, sc 2) 8 times—40 sts.

Rnd 30: (Sc 3, sc2tog) 8 times—32 sts.

Rnd 31: (Sc 1, sc2tog, sc 1) 8 times—24 sts.

Rnd 32: (Sc 1, sc2tog) 8 times—16 sts.

Fasten off, leaving a long tail for sewing. Stuff body firmly, but do not close hole.

If using plastic safety eyes, attach eyes to the front of the body between Rnds 3 and 4. You may wish to remove a bit of stuffing after positioning the eyes to make installing the eye backings easier. For children under 3, sew on crocheted eyes (page 13) or embroider eyes using the bulky black yarn and a tight grouping of satin stitches (page 10).

Using a mattress stitch, bring the edges of the hole in the back of the body together and sew the seam closed in a straight line level with the ch-8 at the beginning of your work.

Muzzle

With B, loosely ch 8.

Rnd 1: Working in back ridge loops, sc 6, sc 3 in next st. Rotate chain so front loops of chain are facing up. Starting in next st, sc 5, sc 2 in next st—16 sts.

Rnd 2: Sc 2 in next st, sc 5, sc 2 in next 3 sts, sc 5, sc 2 in next 2 sts—22 sts.

Rnd 3: Sc 2 in next st, sc 7, sc 2 in next 4 sts, sc 7, sc 2 in next 3 sts—30 sts.

Rnd 4: Sc 30.

Fasten off, leaving a long tail for sewing.

Line up the top edge of the muzzle between the eyes and the bottom edge of the muzzle across the lower edge of the face (around Rnd 5). Sew open edge down with mattress stitch, stuffing muzzle firmly before closing seam.

Ears and Tail (make 2 in B and 1 in A)

With A or B, loosely ch 4.

Row 1: Starting in 2nd ch from hook, sc 3 and turn—3 sts.

Row 2: Ch 1, sc 1, sk 1, sc 1 and turn—2 sts.

Row 3: Ch 1, sc2tog and pm—1 st.

Continue to sc evenly along the side, bottom edge, and opposite side of the ear or tail until you reach the marker. (Sc 1, ch 2, sl st 1) in marked st, fasten off in next st and cut yarn, leaving a long tail for sewing.

Whipstitch the rounded base of the ears to the head about 6 rnds behind the eyes. Sew the pointy end of the tail to the back of the body so the rounded end droops down.

Legs (make 4)

Starting with C, make a 6-st AR.

Rnd 1: Sc 2 in each st around—12 sts.

Cut C, change to B.

Rnd 2: In bl, Sc2tog 6 times—6 sts.

Rnd 3: Sc 6.

Fasten off, leaving a long tail for sewing.

Stuff and mattress stitch the open edges of the legs to the bottom of the body (around Rnds 12–13 for the front legs and Rnds 22–23 for the back legs) with about 8 sts of space between the inside edges of the legs.

NOTE: When sewing the legs to the bottom of the body, leave the yarn tails unsecured until all 4 legs are sewn in place to allow for easier removal and adjustments. Once you are satisfied with the leg placement, fasten off the yarn tails and weave in the ends.

FINISHING: Double a long piece of the bulky black yarn on a tapestry needle. Using the photo as a guide, embroider a "Y" shape onto the front of the muzzle using long stitches. Embroider an eyebrow over each eye.

Weave in any remaining yarn tails.

Preston Pony

Preston Pony, the noble steed, dreams of the rodeo but is willing to slow down and trade a free ride for an apple (or two!)

YARNS

Super Bulky Bernat® Blanket™ Yarn—
(A) #10014 Sand (200yds/185m)
(B) #10430 Purple Plum (50yds/45m)
(C) #10040 Coal (20yds/18m)
(D) #04005 White (10yds/8m)

Bulky Berroco® Comfort®
Chunky—#5734 Liquorice (2yds/2m)

Optional (for child-safe eyes):
Worsted Berroco® Comfort®—#9734
Liquorice. See page 13 for pattern.

NOTIONS

• Size M/N (9.0mm) crochet hook
• Two 21mm black safety eyes
• Large steel tapestry needl
• Scissors
• Polyester fiberfill (12oz/340g)
• *Optional*: Large safety pins for place markers, bamboo straight pins

FINISHED SIZE

13" long, 9" wide, 7" tall

Preston Pony

Body

With A, loosely ch 8.

Rnd 1: Working in back ridge loops, sc 6, sc 3 in next st. Rotate chain so front loops of chain are facing up. Starting in next st, sc 5, sc 2 in next st—16 sts.

Rnd 2: Sc 2 in next st, sc 5, sc 2 in next 3 sts, sc 5, sc 2 in next 2 sts—22 sts.

Rnd 3: Sc 2 in next st, sc 7, sc 2 in next 4 sts, sc 7, sc 2 in next 3 sts—30 sts.

Rnd 4: Sc 2 in next 2 sts, sc 9, sc 2 in next 6 sts, sc 9, sc 2 in next 4 sts—42 sts.

Rnd 5: (Sc 3, sc 2 in next st, sc 3) 6 times—48 sts.

Rnd 6: (Sc 2, sc 2 in next st) 16 times—64 sts.

Rnds 7–8: Sc 64.

Rnd 9: (Sc 2, sc2tog) 16 times—48 sts.

Rnds 10–27: Sc 48.

Rnd 28: (Sc 2, sc2tog, sc 2) 8 times—40 sts.

Rnd 29: (Sc 3, sc2tog) 8 times—32 sts.

Rnd 30: (Sc 1, sc2tog, sc 1) 8 times—24 sts.

Rnd 31: (Sc 1, sc2tog) 8 times—16 sts.

Fasten off, leaving a long tail for sewing. Stuff body firmly, but do not close hole.

If using plastic safety eyes, attach eyes to the front of the body between Rnds 3 and 4. You may wish to remove a bit of stuffing after positioning the eyes to make installing the eye backings easier. For children under 3, sew on crocheted eyes (page 13) or embroider eyes using the bulky black yarn and a tight grouping of satin stitches (page 10).

Using a mattress stitch, bring the edges of the hole in the back of the body together and sew the seam closed in a straight line level with the ch-8 at the beginning of your work.

Muzzle

Starting with D, loosely ch 8.

Rnd 1: Working in back ridge loops, sc 6, sc 3 in next st. Rotate chain so front loops of chain are facing up. Starting in next st, sc 5, sc 2 in next st—16 sts.

Rnd 2: Sc 2 in next st, sc 5, sc 2 in next 3 sts, sc 5, sc 2 in next 2 sts—22 sts.

Rnd 3: Sc 2 in next st, sc 7, sc 2 in next 4 sts, sc 7, sc 2 in next 3 sts—30 sts.

Cut D, change to A.

Rnds 4–5: Sc 30.

Fasten off, leaving a long tail for sewing.

Line up the top edge of the muzzle between the eyes and the bottom edge of the muzzle across the lower edge of the face (around Rnd 5). Sew open edge down with mattress stitch, stuffing muzzle firmly before closing seam.

Blaze Mark

With D, loosely ch 3 and turn.

Row 1: Ch 1, sc 2 and turn—2 sts.

Row 2: Ch 1, sc 2 in next 2 sts and turn—4 sts.

Row 3: Ch 1, sc2tog and turn—2 sts.

Row 4: Ch 1, sc2tog and pm—1 st.

Continue to sc evenly along the side, bottom edge, and opposite side of the blaze mark until you reach the marker. (Sc 1, ch 2, sl st 1) in marked st, fasten off in next st and cut yarn, leaving a long tail for sewing.

Line up bottom edge of blaze mark along the top edge of Rnd 3 of the muzzle. Pin blaze to muzzle and face. With D, backstitch blaze in place.

Nostrils (make 2)

With D, make a 5-st AR but do not join. Cut yarn and pull through current st to fasten off.

Pinch the 1st and 5th sts of the 5-st AR together and secure with a couple of stitches. With the pinched corners pointed toward each other, sew the nostrils to the middle of the muzzle on either side of the blaze with about 6–7 sts between them.

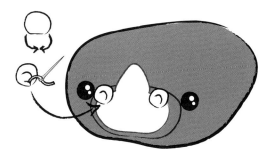

Ears (make 2)

With A, loosely ch 4.

Row 1: Starting in 2nd ch from hook, sc 3 and turn—3 sts.

Row 2: Ch 1, sc 1, sk 1, sc 1 and turn—2 sts.

Row 3: Ch 1, sc2tog and pm—1 st.

Continue to sc evenly along the side, bottom edge, and opposite side of the ear until you reach the marker. (Sc 1, ch 2, sl st 1) in marked st, fasten off in next st and cut yarn, leaving a long tail for sewing.

With A, whipstitch the rounded base of the ears to the head about 4–5 rnds behind the eyes.

Legs (make 4)

Starting with C, make a 6-st AR.

Rnd 1: Sc 2 in each st around—12 sts.

Cut C, change to D.

Rnd 2: In bl, sc2tog 6 times—6 sts.

Cut D, change to A.

Rnd 3: Sc 6.

Fasten off, leaving a long tail for sewing.

Stuff and mattress stitch the open edges of the legs to the bottom of the body (around Rnds 12–13 for the front legs and Rnds 22–23 for the back legs) with about 8 sts of space between the inside edges of the legs.

NOTE: When sewing the legs to the bottom of the body, leave the yarn tails unsecured until all 4 legs are sewn in place to allow for easier removal and adjustments. Once you are satisfied with the leg placement, fasten off the yarn tails and weave in the ends.

Tail

With B, make a 5-st AR.

Rnd 1: (Sl 1, ch 12. Starting in 2nd ch from hook and working in back ridge loops, sl st 11, sl st in st at base of ch-12) in each st around.

Fasten off, leaving a long tail for sewing.

Stitch a running stitch along the base stitches of Rnd 1 and pull to cinch Rnd 1 closed. Whipstitch base of tail to the back of the body.

Mane

With B, loosely ch 21.

Starting in 2nd ch from hook and working in back ridge loops (sl 1, ch 8. Starting in 2nd ch from hook and working in back ridge loops, sl st 7, sl st in st at base of ch-8) in each ch to end.

Fold the ch-21 in half so that the 1st and last ch line up with each other. Sew the folded chain edges together with a whipstitch, taking care not to get the mane twisted as you sew.

Backstitch the whipstitched center of the mane to the top of the head, starting at the ears and ending around the mid-back.

FINISHING: Double a long piece of the bulky black yarn on a tapestry needle and embroider an eyebrow over each eye.

Weave in any remaining yarn tails.

Connie Cow

Captivating Connie Cow is udderly adorable with her soft pink nose, cute little horns, and heart-shaped spots.

YARNS

Super Bulky Bernat® Blanket™ Yarn—
(A) #04005 White (180yds/165m)
(B) #12003 School Bus Yellow
   (30yds/27m)
(C) #04758 Shell Pink (10yds/9m)
(D) #10040 Coal (20yds/18m)

Bulky Berroco® Comfort®
Chunky—#5734 Liquorice (2yds/2m)

Optional (for child-safe eyes):
Worsted Berroco® Comfort®—#9734
Liquorice. See page 13 for pattern.

NOTIONS

- Size M/N (9.0mm) crochet hook
- Two 21mm black safety eyes
- Large steel tapestry needle
- Scissors
- Polyester fiberfill (12oz/340g)
- *Optional:* Large safety pins for place markers, bamboo straight pins

FINISHED SIZE

13" long, 9" wide, 7" tall

Connie Cow

Body

With A, loosely ch 8.

Rnd 1: Working in back ridge loops, sc 6, sc 3 in next st. Rotate chain so front loops of chain are facing up. Starting in next st, sc 5, sc 2 in next st—16 sts.

Rnd 2: Sc 2 in next st, sc 5, sc 2 in next 3 sts, sc 5, sc 2 in next 2 sts—22 sts.

Rnd 3: Sc 2 in next st, sc 7, sc 2 in next 4 sts, sc 7, sc 2 in next 3 sts—30 sts.

Rnd 4: Sc 2 in next 2 sts, sc 9, sc 2 in next 6 sts, sc 9, sc 2 in next 4 sts—42 sts.

Rnd 5: (Sc 3, sc 2 in next st, sc 3) 6 times—48 sts.

Rnd 6: (Sc 2, sc 2 in next st) 16 times—64 sts.

Rnds 7–8: Sc 64.

Rnd 9: (Sc 2, sc2tog) 16 times—48 sts.

Rnds 10–27: Sc 48.

Rnd 28: (Sc 2, sc2tog, sc 2) 8 times—40 sts. **Rnd 29:** (Sc 3, sc2tog) 8 times—32 sts.

Rnd 30: (Sc 1, sc2tog, sc 1) 8 times—24 sts.

Rnd 31: (Sc 1, sc2tog) 8 times—16 sts.

Fasten off, leaving a long tail for sewing. Stuff body firmly, but do not close hole.

If using plastic safety eyes, attach eyes to the front of the body between Rnds 3 and 4. You may wish to remove a bit of stuffing after positioning the eyes to make installing the eye backings easier. For children under 3, sew on crocheted eyes (page 13) or embroider eyes using the bulky black yarn and a tight grouping of satin stitches (page 10).

Using a mattress stitch, bring the edges of the hole in the back of the body together and sew the seam closed in a straight line level with the ch-8 at the beginning of your work.

Muzzle

Starting with C, loosely ch 11.

Rnd 1: Working in back ridge loops, sc 9, sc 3 in next st. Rotate chain so front loops of chain are facing up. Starting in next st, sc 8, sc 2 in next st—22 sts.

Rnd 2: Sc 2 in next st, sc 7, sc 2 in next 4 sts, sc 7, sc 2 in next 3 sts—30 sts.

Rnd 3: Sc 2 in next 2 sts, sc 9, sc 2 in next 6 sts, sc 9, sc 2 in next 4 sts—42 sts.

Cut C, change to A.

Rnd 4: Sc 42.

Rnd 5: (Sc 5, sc2tog) 6 times—36 sts.

Fasten off, leaving a long tail for sewing.

Line up the top edge of the muzzle between the eyes and the bottom edge of the muzzle across the lower edge of the face (around Rnd 5). With A, sew open edge down with mattress stitch, stuffing muzzle firmly before closing seam.

Nostrils (make 2)

With C, make a 5-st AR but do not join. Turn and work semicircle shape in rows.

Row 1: Ch 1, sl st 5 and fasten off.

Pinch the corners of nostril together and secure with a couple of stitches. With the pinched corners pointed down, whipstitch the back side of the nostril to the upper half of the pink portion of the muzzle.

Ears (make 2)

With A, loosely ch 4.

Row 1: Starting in 2nd ch from hook, sc 3 and turn—3 sts.

Row 2: Ch 1, sc 1, sk 1, sc 1 and turn—2 sts.

Row 3: Ch 1, sc2tog and pm—1 st.

Continue to sc evenly along the side, bottom edge, and opposite side of the ear until you reach the marker. (Sc 1, ch 2, sl st 1) in marked st, fasten off in next st and cut yarn, leaving a long tail for sewing.

With A, whipstitch the rounded base of the ears to the head about 4–5 rnds behind the eyes.

Horns (make 2)

With B, make a 4-st AR.

Rnd 1: Sc 4.

Rnd 2: (Sc 1, sc 2 in next st) 2 times—6 sts.

Rnd 3: Sc 6.

Fasten off, leaving a long tail for sewing.

Stuff horns lightly. With B, mattress stitch open edges of horns to top of head between the ears.

Heart Spots (make 5)

With D, make a 7-st AR but do not join. Turn and work semicircle shape in rows.

Row 1: Ch 1, hdc 2 in next st, sc 1, sl st 1, (sl st 1, ch 1, sl st 1) in next st, sl st 1, sc 1, hdc 2 in next st—10 sts.

Fasten off in current st, leaving a long tail for sewing.

With D, backstitch along the edges to sew heart spots to the back and sides of the body.

Legs (make 4)

Starting with B, make a 6-st AR.

Rnd 1: Sc 2 in each st around—12 sts.

Cut B, change to A.

Rnd 2: In bl, sc2tog 6 times—6 sts.

Rnd 3: Sc 6.

Fasten off, leaving a long tail for sewing.

Stuff and mattress stitch the open edges of the legs to the bottom of the body (around Rnds 12–13 for the front legs and Rnds 22–23 for the back legs) with about 8 sts of space between the inside edges of the legs.

NOTE: When sewing the legs to the bottom of the body, leave the yarn tails unsecured until all 4 legs are sewn in place to allow for easier removal and adjustments. Once you are satisfied with the leg placement, fasten off the yarn tails and weave in the ends.

Udder

With C, make a 6-st AR.

Rnd 1: Sc 2 in each st around—12 sts.

Rnd 2: (Sc 3, hdc 2 in next 3 sts) 2 times—18 sts.

Cut yarn and fasten off in next st, leaving a long tail for sewing.

Teats (make 4)

With C, make a 5-st AR.

Cut yarn and fasten off in next st, leaving a long tail for sewing.

Mattress stitch teats to surface of udder.

Mattress stitch open edge of udder to underside of body directly in front of the back legs. Stuff lightly before closing seam.

Tail

With A, make a 4-st AR.

Row 1: Sc 2 and turn, leaving remaining 2 sts unworked.

Rows 2–3: Ch 1, sc 2 and turn.

Fasten off, leaving a long tail for sewing.

Tail Hair

Row 1: With D, (sl st 1, ch 1, sc 2) in 1st unworked st of tail. Sc 2 in next unworked st of tail and turn—4 sts.

Row 2: Ch 1, (sl st 1, ch 2, sl st) in next 4 sts and fasten off.

With A, sew the long edges of Rows 1–3 of the tail together. With D, sew only the ends of Row 1 of the tail hair section together. Attach base of tail to back of body.

FINISHING: Double a long piece of the bulky black yarn on a tapestry needle and embroider an eyebrow over each eye.

Weave in any remaining yarn tails.

Henry Hippo

Happy Henry Hippo looks great in any color.
Hip, hip, hooray for colorful, huggable hippos!

YARNS

Super Bulky Bernat® Blanket™ Yarn—
(A) #04310 Baby Lilac (200yds/180m)
(B) #04005 White (5yds/4m)

Bulky Berroco® Comfort®
Chunky—#5734 Liquorice (2yds/2m)

Optional (for child-safe eyes):
Worsted Berroco® Comfort®—#9734
Liquorice. See page 13 for pattern.

NOTIONS

- Size M/N (9.0mm) crochet hook
- Two 21mm black safety eyes
- Large steel tapestry needle
- Scissors
- Polyester fiberfill (12oz/340g)
- *Optional*: Large safety pins for place markers, bamboo straight pins

FINISHED SIZE

13" long, 9" wide, 7" tall

Henry Hippo

Body

With A, loosely ch 8.

Rnd 1: Working in back ridge loops, sc 6, sc 3 in next st. Rotate chain so front loops of chain are facing up. Starting in next st, sc 5, sc 2 in next st—16 sts.

Rnd 2: Sc 2 in next st, sc 5, sc 2 in next 3 sts, sc 5, sc 2 in next 2 sts—22 sts.

Rnd 3: Sc 2 in next st, sc 7, sc 2 in next 4 sts, sc 7, sc 2 in next 3 sts—30 sts.

Rnd 4: Sc 2 in next 2 sts, sc 9, sc 2 in next 6 sts, sc 9, sc 2 in next 4 sts—42 sts.

Rnd 5: (Sc 3, sc 2 in next st, sc 3) 6 times—48 sts.

Rnd 6: (Sc 2, sc 2 in next st) 16 times—64 sts.

Rnds 7–8: Sc 64.

Rnd 9: (Sc 2, sc2tog) 16 times—48 sts.

Rnds 10–27: Sc 48.

Rnd 28: (Sc 2, sc2tog, sc 2) 8 times—40 sts.

Rnd 29: (Sc 3, sc2tog) 8 times—32 sts.

Rnd 30: (Sc 1, sc2tog, sc 1) 8 times—24 sts.

Rnd 31: (Sc 1, sc2tog) 8 times—16 sts.

Fasten off, leaving a long tail for sewing. Stuff body firmly, but do not close hole.

If using plastic safety eyes, attach eyes to the front of the body between Rnds 3 and 4. You may wish to remove a bit of stuffing after positioning the eyes to make installing the eye backings easier. For children under 3, sew on crocheted eyes (page 13) or embroider eyes using the bulky black yarn and a tight grouping of satin stitches (page 10).

Using a mattress stitch, bring the edges of the hole in the back of the body together and sew the seam closed in a straight line level with the ch-8 at the beginning of your work.

Muzzle

With A, loosely ch 11.

Rnd 1: Working in back ridge loops, sc 9, sc 3 in next st. Rotate chain so front loops of chain are facing up. Starting in next st, sc 8, sc 2 in next st—22 sts.

Rnd 2: Sc 2 in next st, sc 7, sc 2 in next 4 sts, sc 7, sc 2 in next 3 sts—30 sts.

Rnd 3: Sc 2 in next 2 sts, sc 9, sc 2 in next 6 sts, sc 9, sc 2 in next 4 sts—42 sts.

Rnd 4: Sc 42.

Rnd 5: (Sc 5, sc2tog) 6 times—36 sts.

Fasten off, leaving a long tail for sewing.

Line up the top edge of the muzzle between the eyes and the bottom edge of the muzzle across the lower edge of the face (around Rnd 5). Sew open edge down with mattress stitch, stuffing muzzle firmly before closing seam.

With A, draw a long stitch out from the front of the muzzle and into the bottom back edge of the muzzle before drawing the yarn out through the starting point in the center of the muzzle again. Repeat 2–3 times, pulling tightly to shape the muzzle.

Nostrils (make 2)

With A, make a 5-st AR. Do not join. Turn and work semicircle shape in rows.

Row 1: Ch 1, sl st 5 and fasten off, leaving a long tail for sewing.

Pinch the corners of nostril together and secure with a couple of stitches. Sew the pinched corner of the nostril to the upper half of the muzzle 2–3 rnds in front of the eyes.

Teeth (make 2)

With B, make a 5-st AR.

Rnd 1: In bl, sc 5.

Cut and fasten off, leaving a long tail for sewing.

Flatten open edge of tooth and whipstitch seam closed. Sew closed edge of teeth to bottom of muzzle.

Ears and Tail (make 3)

With A, loosely ch 4.

Row 1: Starting in 2nd ch from hook, sc 3 and turn—3 sts.

Row 2: Ch 1, sc 1, sk 1, sc 1 and turn—2 sts.

Row 3: Ch 1, sc2tog and pm—1 st.

Continue to sc evenly along the side, bottom edge, and opposite side of the ear or tail until you reach the marker. (Sc 1, ch 2, sl st 1) in marked st, fasten off in next st and cut yarn, leaving a long tail for sewing.

Using a whipstitch, sew the pointy end of the ears to the head 4 rnds behind the eyes and the pointy end of the tail to the back of the body so the rounded end of the tail hangs down.

Legs (make 4)

With A, make a 6-st AR.

Rnd 1: Sc 2 in each st around—12 sts.

Rnd 2: In bl, sc2tog 6 times—6 sts.

Fasten off, leaving a long tail for sewing.

Stuff and mattress stitch the open edges of the legs to the bottom of the body (around Rnds 12–13 for the front legs and Rnds 22–23 for the back legs) with about 8 sts of space between the inside edges of the legs.

NOTE: When sewing the legs to the bottom of the body, leave the yarn tails unsecured until all 4 legs are sewn in place to allow for easier removal and adjustments. Once you are satisfied with the leg placement, fasten off the yarn tails and weave in the ends.

FINISHING: Double a long piece of the bulky black yarn on a tapestry needle and embroider an eyebrow over each eye.

Weave in any remaining yarn tails.

Polly Panda

What's black and white and squishy all over?
Pretty, pillowy Polly Panda, of course!

YARNS

Super Bulky Bernat® Blanket™ Yarn—
(A) #04005 White (150yds/165m)
(B) #10040 Coal (75yds/68m)

Bulky Berroco® Comfort®
Chunky—#5734 Liquorice (2yds/2m)

Optional (for child-safe eyes and nose):
Worsted Berroco® Comfort®—#9734
Liquorice. See page 13 for patterns.

NOTIONS

- Size M/N (9.0mm) crochet hook
- Two 21mm black safety eyes and one 29mm black triangle safety nose
- Large steel tapestry needle
- Scissors
- Polyester fiberfill (12oz/340g)
- *Optional*: Large safety pins for place markers, bamboo straight pins

FINISHED SIZE

13" long, 9" wide, 7" tall

Polly Panda

Body

Starting with A, loosely ch 8.

Rnd 1: Working in back ridge loops, sc 6, sc 3 in next st. Rotate chain so front loops of chain are facing up. Starting in next st, sc 5, sc 2 in next st—16 sts.

Rnd 2: Sc 2 in next st, sc 5, sc 2 in next 3 sts, sc 5, sc 2 in next 2 sts—22 sts.

Rnd 3: Sc 2 in next st, sc 7, sc 2 in next 4 sts, sc 7, sc 2 in next 3 sts—30 sts.

Rnd 4: Sc 2 in next 2 sts, sc 9, sc 2 in next 6 sts, sc 9, sc 2 in next 4 sts—42 sts.

Rnd 5: (Sc 3, sc 2 in next st, sc 3) 6 times—48 sts.

Rnd 6: (Sc 2, sc 2 in next st) 16 times—64 sts.

Rnds 7–8: Sc 64.

Rnd 9: (Sc 2, sc2tog) 16 times—48 sts.

Change to B.

Refer to Jogless Color Changes on page 7 for tips on how to create smoother stripe transitions from one round to the next!

Rnds 10–16: Sc 48.

Change to A.

Rnds 17–27: Sc 48.

Rnd 28: (Sc 2, sc2tog, sc 2) 8 times—40 sts.

Rnd 29: (Sc 3, sc2tog) 8 times—32 sts.

Rnd 30: (Sc 1, sc2tog, sc 1) 8 times—24 sts.

Rnd 31: (Sc 1, sc2tog) 8 times—16 sts.

Fasten off, leaving a long tail for sewing. Stuff body firmly. Using a mattress stitch, bring the edges of the hole in the back of the body together and sew the seam closed in a straight line level with the ch-8 at the beginning of your work.

With A, draw a long stitch out from the middle of the ch-8 in the center of the face and into the bottom of the head (around Rnd 6) before drawing the yarn out through the starting point in the center of the face again. Repeat 2–3 times, pulling tightly to shape the cheeks.

Muzzle

With A, make a 7-st AR.

Rnd 1: Sc 2 in each st around—14 sts.

Rnd 2: (Sl st 3, hdc 2 in next 4 sts) 2 times—22 sts.

Fasten off, leaving a long tail for sewing.

With the hdc increases oriented on the left and right sides of the muzzle, attach safety nose between Rnds 1 and 2 directly above the center of the muzzle.

Attach open edge of muzzle to the front of the body with a mattress stitch and stuff before closing seam. For children under 3, sew on crocheted nose (page 13) or embroider nose using the bulky black yarn and a tight grouping of satin stitches (page 10) after you have attached the muzzle to the front of the face.

Eye Spots (make 2)

With B, make a 6-st AR.

Rnd 1: Sc 1, sc 2 in next st, hdc 2 in next 2 sts, sc 2 in next st, sc 1—10 sts.

Fasten off, leaving a long tail for sewing.

If using plastic safety eyes, insert the eye posts into the middle of the eye spots and secure the backings.

For children under 3, sew on crocheted eyes (page 13) or embroider on eyes using the bulky black yarn and a satin stitch (page 10) to the center of the eye spots.

There will be a slight taper to Rnd 1 of the eye spots where the rnd starts and ends with a sc st. Position the taper to point toward the top edge of the muzzle. With B, sew the edges of the eye spots down using a backstitch.

Ears (make 2)

With B, make a 6-st AR but do not join. Turn and work semicircle shape in rows.

Row 1: Ch 1, sc 1 in each st to end—6 sts.

Sl st into ch 1 at beg of Row 1 to pinch bottom of ear together. Fasten off.

Whipstitch pinched end of ear to head above the eye spots, 1 rnd before the black body stripe.

Tail

With B, make a 4-st AR.

Rnd 1: Sc 2 in each st around—8 sts.

Rnd 2: Sc 8.

Fasten off, leaving a long tail for sewing.

Stuff tail and sew open edge to back of body using a mattress stitch.

Legs (make 4)

With B, make a 6-st AR.

Rnd 1: Sc 2 in each st around—12 sts.

Rnd 2: Sc2tog 6 times—6 sts.

Fasten off, leaving a long tail for sewing.

Stuff and mattress stitch the open edges of the legs to the bottom of the body (around Rnds 12–13 for the front legs and Rnds 22–23 for the back legs) with about 8 sts of space between the inside edges of the legs.

NOTE: When sewing the legs to the bottom of the body, leave the yarn tails unsecured until all 4 legs are sewn in place to allow for easier removal and adjustments. Once you are satisfied with the leg placement, fasten off the yarn tails and weave in the ends.

FINISHING: Weave in any remaining yarn tails.

Lucas Lion

Lucas Lion thinks it would be fun to be king of the jungle, but he'd be just as happy being crowned king of the couch.

YARNS

Super Bulky Bernat® Blanket™ Yarn—
(A) #12003 School Bus Yellow
   (200yds/180m)
(B) #04008 Vanilla (50yds/45m)
(C) #10630 Pumpkin Spice (25yds/22m)

Bulky Berroco® Comfort®
Chunky—#5734 Liquorice (2yds/2m)

Optional (for child-safe eyes and nose):
Worsted Berroco® Comfort®—#9734
Liquorice and #9723 Rosebud.
See page 13 for patterns.

NOTIONS

- Size M/N (9.0mm) crochet hook
- Two 21mm black safety eyes and one 29mm pink heart safety nose
- Large steel tapestry needle
- Scissors
- Polyester fiberfill (12oz/340g)
- *Optional*: Large safety pins for place markers, bamboo straight pins

FINISHED SIZE

13" long, 9" wide, 7" tall

Lucas Lion

Body

With A, loosely ch 8.

Rnd 1: Working in back ridge loops, sc 6, sc 3 in next st. Rotate chain so front loops of chain are facing up. Starting in next st, sc 5, sc 2 in next st—16 sts.

Rnd 2: Sc 2 in next st, sc 5, sc 2 in next 3 sts, sc 5, sc 2 in next 2 sts—22 sts.

Rnd 3: Sc 2 in next st, sc 7, sc 2 in next 4 sts, sc 7, sc 2 in next 3 sts—30 sts.

Rnd 4: Sc 2 in next 2 sts, sc 9, sc 2 in next 6 sts, sc 9, sc 2 in next 4 sts—42 sts.

Rnd 5: (Sc 3, sc 2 in next st, sc 3) 6 times—48 sts.

Rnd 6: (Sc 2, sc 2 in next st) 16 times—64 sts.

Rnds 7–8: Sc 64.

Rnd 9: (Sc 2, sc2tog) 16 times—48 sts.

Rnds 10–27: Sc 48.

Rnd 28: (Sc 2, sc2tog, sc 2) 8 times—40 sts.

Rnd 29: (Sc 3, sc2tog) 8 times—32 sts.

Rnd 30: (Sc 1, sc2tog, sc 1) 8 times—24 sts.

Rnd 31: (Sc 1, sc2tog) 8 times—16 sts.

Fasten off, leaving a long tail for sewing. Stuff body firmly, but do not close hole.

If using plastic safety eyes, attach eyes to the front of the body between Rnds 3 and 4. You may wish to remove a bit of stuffing after positioning the eyes to make installing the eye backings easier. For children under 3, sew on crocheted eyes (page 13) or embroider eyes using the bulky black yarn and a tight grouping of satin stitches (page 10).

Using a mattress stitch, bring the edges of the hole in the back of the body together and sew the seam closed in a straight line level with the ch-8 at the beginning of your work.

With A, draw a long stitch out from the middle of the ch-8 in the center of the face and into the bottom of the head (around Rnd 6) before drawing the yarn out through the starting point in the center of the face again. Repeat 2–3 times, pulling tightly to shape the cheeks.

Muzzle

With B, make a 7-st AR.

Rnd 1: Sc 2 in each st around—14 sts.

Rnd 2: (Sl st 3, hdc 2 in next 4 sts) 2 times—22 sts.

Fasten off, leaving a long tail for sewing.

With the hdc increases oriented on the left and right sides of the muzzle, attach safety nose between Rnds 1 and 2 directly above the center of the muzzle.

Attach open edge of muzzle to the front of the body with a mattress stitch and stuff before closing seam. For children under 3, sew on crocheted nose (page 13) or embroider nose using the bulky pink yarn and a tight grouping of satin stitches (page 10) after you have attached the muzzle to the front of the face.

To add a lip cleft below a plastic safety nose, tie the middle of an 18–20" strand of the bulky black yarn around the post of the nose. Thread your tapestry needle with the yarn tails and draw a long stitch down over the front of the muzzle, and fasten off beneath the muzzle to create the lip cleft detail.

NOTE: The same long stitch can also be embroidered onto the muzzle when using child-safe nose options (page 13).

Ears (make 2)

With A, loosely ch 4.

Row 1: Starting in 2nd ch from hook, sc 3 and turn—3 sts.

Row 2: Ch 1, sc 1, sk 1, sc 1 and turn—2 sts.

Row 3: Ch 1, sc2tog and pm—1 st.

Continue to sc evenly along the side, bottom edge, and opposite side of the ear until you reach the marker. (Sc 1, ch 2, sl st 1) in marked st, fasten off in next st and cut yarn, leaving a long tail for sewing.

Using a whipstitch, sew the rounded base of the ears to the head 4 rnds behind the eyes.

Belly

With B, loosely ch 8.

Rnd 1: Working in back ridge loops, sc 6, sc 3 in next st. Rotate chain so front loops of chain are facing up. Starting in next st, sc 5, sc 2 in next st—16 sts.

Rnd 2: Sc 2 in next st, sc 5, sc 2 in next 3 sts, sc 5, sc 2 in next 2 sts—22 sts.

Rnd 3: Sc 2 in next st, sc 7, sc 2 in next 4 sts, sc 7, sc 2 in next 3 sts—30 sts.

Rnd 4: Sc 2 in next 2 sts, sc 9, sc 2 in next 6 sts, sc 9, sc 2 in next 4 sts—42 sts.

Rnd 5: (Sc 3, sc 2 in next st, sc 3) 6 times—48 sts.

Rnd 6: (Sc 2, sc 2 in next st) 16 times—64 sts.

Fasten off, leaving a long tail for sewing.

Using a backstitch, sew the edge of the belly to the bottom of the body.

Tail

Starting with C, make a 4-st AR.

Rnd 1: Sc 2 in each st around—8 sts.

Rnd 2: (Sc 1, sc 2 in next st) 4 times—12 sts.

Cut C, change to A.

Rnd 3: Sc2tog 6 times—6 sts.

Rnd 4: (Sc 1, sc2tog) 2 times—4 sts.

Rnds 5–9: Sc 4.

Fasten off, leaving a long tail for sewing.

Stuff tip of tail. Using a mattress stitch, sew open edge of tail to back of body.

Legs (make 4)

Starting with B, make a 6-st AR.

Rnd 1: Sc 2 in each st around—12 sts.

Cut B, change to A.

Rnd 2: Sc2tog 6 times—6 sts.

Rnd 3: Sc 6.

Fasten off, leaving a long tail for sewing.

Stuff and mattress stitch the open edges of the legs to the bottom of the body (around Rnds 12–13 for the front legs and Rnds 22–23 for the back legs) with about 8 sts of space between the inside edges of the legs. The legs may overlap the belly slightly.

NOTE: When sewing the legs to the bottom of the body, leave the yarn tails unsecured until all 4 legs are sewn in place to allow for easier removal and adjustments. Once you are satisfied with the leg placement, fasten off the yarn tails and weave in the ends.

FINISHING: Double a long piece of the bulky black yarn on a tapestry needle and embroider an eyebrow over each eye.

Weave in any remaining yarn tails.

Mane (Optional)

With C, working in the rnd directly in front of the ears and starting in the surface stitch below the lion's left cheek, (sl st 1, ch 1, sc 1) in surface stitch to rejoin yarn. *Ch 5, starting in 2nd ch from hook, sc 3 in next 4 chs, sl st 1 in next surface stitch, sc 1 in next surface stitch. Repeat from * as many times as needed, working the mane into rnd directly in front of the ears from the lower left cheek to the lower right cheek, and ending with the sl st 1. Fasten off yarn.

Refer to Working in Surface Stitches on page 8 for tips on how to crochet into the surface of your work!

Taylor Tiger

Don't let the fierce stripes fool you, Taylor Tiger is all about hunting down nature shows from the comfort of her favorite chair.

YARNS

Super Bulky Bernat® Blanket™ Yarn—
(A) #12002 Carrot Orange (200yds/180m)
(B) #10040 Coal (75yds/68m)
(C) #04005 White (50yds/45m)

Bulky Berroco® Comfort®
Chunky—#5734 Liquorice (2yds/2m)

Optional (for child-safe eyes and nose):
Worsted Berroco® Comfort®—#9734
Liquorice and #9723 Rosebud.
See page 13 for patterns.

NOTIONS

- Size M/N (9.0mm) crochet hook
- Two 21mm black safety eyes and one 29mm pink heart safety nose
- Large steel tapestry needle
- Scissors
- Polyester fiberfill (12oz/340g)
- *Optional:* Large safety pins for place markers, bamboo straight pins

FINISHED SIZE

13" long, 9" wide, 7" tall

Taylor Tiger

Body

Starting with A, loosely ch 8.

Rnd 1: Working in back ridge loops, sc 6, sc 3 in next st. Rotate chain so front loops of chain are facing up. Starting in next st, sc 5, sc 2 in next st—16 sts.

Rnd 2: Sc 2 in next st, sc 5, sc 2 in next 3 sts, sc 5, sc 2 in next 2 sts—22 sts.

Rnd 3: Sc 2 in next st, sc 7, sc 2 in next 4 sts, sc 7, sc 2 in next 3 sts—30 sts.

Rnd 4: Sc 2 in next 2 sts, sc 9, sc 2 in next 6 sts, sc 9, sc 2 in next 4 sts—42 sts.

Rnd 5: (Sc 3, sc 2 in next st, sc 3) 6 times—48 sts.

Rnd 6: (Sc 2, sc 2 in next st) 16 times—64 sts.

Rnds 7–8: Sc 64.

Rnd 9: (Sc 2, sc2tog) 16 times—48 sts.

Rnds 10–27: Change to B. Alt 2 rnds in B and 2 rnds in A, ending with 2 rnds of B.

Refer to Jogless Color Changes on page 7 for tips on how to create smoother stripe transitions from one round to the next!

Cut B and continue in A.

Rnd 28: (Sc 2, sc2tog, sc 2) 8 times—40 sts.

Rnd 29: (Sc 3, sc2tog) 8 times—32 sts.

Rnd 30: (Sc 1, sc2tog, sc 1) 8 times—24 sts.

Rnd 31: (Sc 1, sc2tog) 8 times—16 sts.

Fasten off, leaving a long tail for sewing. Stuff body firmly. Using a mattress stitch, bring the edges of the hole in the back of the body together and sew the seam closed in a straight line level with the ch-8 at the beginning of your work.

With A, draw a long stitch out from the middle of the ch-8 in the center of the face and into the bottom of the head (around Rnd 6) before drawing the yarn out through the starting point in the center of the face again. Repeat 2–3 times, pulling tightly to shape the cheeks.

Muzzle

With C, make a 7-st AR.

Rnd 1: Sc 2 in each st around—14 sts.

Rnd 2: (Sl st 3, hdc 2 in next 4 sts) 2 times—22 sts.

Fasten off, leaving a long tail for sewing.

With the hdc increases oriented on the left and right sides of the muzzle, attach safety nose between Rnds 1 and 2 directly above the center of the muzzle.

Attach open edge of muzzle to the front of the body with a mattress stitch and stuff before closing seam. For children under 3, sew on crocheted nose (page 13) or embroider nose using the bulky pink yarn and a tight grouping of satin stitches (page 10) after you have attached the muzzle to the front of the face.

To add a lip cleft below a plastic safety nose, tie the middle of an 18–20" strand of the bulky black yarn around the post of the nose. Thread your tapestry needle with the yarn tails and draw a long stitch down over the front of the muzzle, and fasten off beneath the muzzle to create the lip cleft detail.

NOTE: The same long stitch can also be embroidered onto the muzzle when using child-safe nose options (page 13).

Eye Spots (make 2)

With C, make a 6-st AR.

Rnd 1: Sc 1, sc 2 in next st, hdc 2 in next 2 sts, sc 2 in next st, sc 1—10 sts.

Fasten off, leaving a long tail for sewing.

If using plastic safety eyes, insert the eye posts into the middle of the eye spots and secure the backings.

For children under 3, sew on crocheted eyes (page 13) or embroider on eyes using the bulky black yarn and a satin stitch (page 10) to the center of the eye spots.

There will be a slight taper to Rnd 1 of the eye spots where the rnd starts and ends with a sc st. Position the taper to point toward the top edge of the muzzle. With C, sew the edges of the eye spots down using a backstitch.

Whiskers (make 2)

With C, loosely ch 7.

Row 1: Starting in 2nd ch from hook, (sl st 1, ch 3. Starting in 2nd ch from hook, sl st 2, sl st 1 in next ch) 3 times. Fasten off yarn.

Whipstitch flat edge of whiskers to the sides of the face in front of the first black stripe.

Ears (make 2)

Starting with A, loosely ch 4.

Row 1: Starting in 2nd ch from hook, sc 3 and turn—3 sts.

Row 2: Ch 1, sc 1, sk 1, sc 1 and turn—2 sts.

Row 3: Ch 1, sc2tog and pm—1 st.

Continue to sc evenly along the side, bottom edge, and opposite side of the ear until you reach the marker. Cut A and change to B. In B, (sl st 1, ch 2, sl st 1) in marked st, fasten off in next st and cut yarn, leaving a long tail for sewing.

Using a whipstitch, sew the rounded base of the ears to the head 4 rnds behind the eyes, right in front of the first black stripe.

Belly

In C, loosely ch 8.

Rnd 1: Working in back ridge loops, sc 6, sc 3 in next st. Rotate chain so front loops of chain are facing up. Starting in next st, sc 5, sc 2 in next st—16 sts.

Rnd 2: Sc 2 in next st, sc 5, sc 2 in next 3 sts, sc 5, sc 2 in next 2 sts—22 sts.

Rnd 3: Sc 2 in next st, sc 7, sc 2 in next 4 sts, sc 7, sc 2 in next 3 sts—30 sts.

Rnd 4: Sc 2 in next 2 sts, sc 9, sc 2 in next 6 sts, sc 9, sc 2 in next 4 sts—42 sts.

Rnd 5: (Sc 3, sc 2 in next st, sc 3) 6 times—48 sts.

Rnd 6: (Sc 2, sc 2 in next st) 16 times—64 sts.

Fasten off, leaving a long tail for sewing.

Using a backstitch, sew the edge of the belly to the bottom of the body.

Tail

Starting with C, make a 6-st AR.

Rnd 1: Sc 2 in each st around—12 sts.

Cut C, change to B.

Rnd 2: (Sc 2, sc2tog) 3 times—9 sts.

Rnd 3: Sc 9.

Change to A.

Rnd 4: (Sc 1, sc2tog) 3 times—6 sts.

Rnd 5: Sc 6.

Change to B.

Rnds 6–7: Sc 6.

Cut B, change to A.

Rnds 8–9: Sc 6.

Fasten off, leaving a long tail for sewing.

Stuff tail. Using a mattress stitch, sew open edge of tail to back of body.

Legs (make 4)

Starting with C, make a 6-st AR.

Rnd 1: Sc 2 in each st around—12 sts.

Cut C, change to B.

Rnd 2: Sc2tog 6 times—6 sts.

Cut B, change to A.

Rnd 3: Sc 6.

Fasten off, leaving a long tail for sewing.

Stuff and mattress stitch the open edges of the legs to the bottom of the body (around Rnds 12–13 for the front legs and Rnds 22–23 for the back legs) with about 8 sts of space between the inside edges of the legs. The legs may overlap the belly slightly.

NOTE: When sewing the legs to the bottom of the body, leave the yarn tails unsecured until all 4 legs are sewn in place to allow for easier removal and adjustments. Once you are satisfied with the leg placement, fasten off the yarn tails and weave in the ends.

FINISHING: Weave in any remaining yarn tails.

Ella Elephant

Ella, the plushie, peanut-loving pachyderm, is the perfect pal to have if you need a reminder when it's lunchtime.

YARNS

Super Bulky Bernat® Blanket™ Yarn—
(A) #10046 Pale Grey (200yds/180m)
(B) #10040 Coal (5yds/68m)
(C) #04008 Vanilla (25yds/22m)

Bulky Berroco® Comfort® Chunky—#5734 Liquorice (2yds/2m)

Optional (for child-safe eyes): Worsted Berroco® Comfort®—#9734 Liquorice. See page 13 for pattern.

NOTIONS

- Size M/N (9.0mm) crochet hook
- Two 21mm black safety eyes
- Large steel tapestry needle
- Scissors
- Polyester fiberfill (12oz/340g)
- *Optional*: Large safety pins for place markers, bamboo straight pins

FINISHED SIZE

13" long, 9" wide, 7" tall

Ella Elephant

Body

With A, loosely ch 8.

Rnd 1: Working in back ridge loops, sc 6, sc 3 in next st. Rotate chain so front loops of chain are facing up. Starting in next st, sc 5, sc 2 in next st—16 sts.

Rnd 2: Sc 2 in next st, sc 5, sc 2 in next 3 sts, sc 5, sc 2 in next 2 sts—22 sts.

Rnd 3: Sc 2 in next st, sc 7, sc 2 in next 4 sts, sc 7, sc 2 in next 3 sts—30 sts.

Rnd 4: Sc 2 in next 2 sts, sc 9, sc 2 in next 6 sts, sc 9, sc 2 in next 4 sts—42 sts.

Rnd 5: (Sc 3, sc 2 in next st, sc 3) 6 times—48 sts.

Rnd 6: (Sc 2, sc 2 in next st) 16 times—64 sts.

Rnds 7–8: Sc 64.

Rnd 9: (Sc 2, sc2tog) 16 times—48 sts.

Rnds 10–27: Sc 48.

Rnd 28: (Sc 2, sc2tog, sc 2) 8 times—40 sts.

Rnd 29: (Sc 3, sc2tog) 8 times—32 sts.

Rnd 30: (Sc 1, sc2tog, sc 1) 8 times—24 sts.

Rnd 31: (Sc 1, sc2tog) 8 times—16 sts.

Fasten off, leaving a long tail for sewing. Stuff body firmly, but do not close hole.

If using plastic safety eyes, attach eyes to the front of the body between Rnds 3 and 4. You may wish to remove a bit of stuffing after positioning the eyes to make installing the eye backings easier. For children under 3, sew on crocheted eyes (page 13) or embroider eyes using the bulky black yarn and a tight grouping of satin stitches (page 10).

Using a mattress stitch, bring the edges of the hole in the back of the body together and sew the seam closed in a straight line level with the ch-8 at the beginning of your work.

With A, draw a long stitch out from the middle of the ch-8 in the center of the face and into the bottom of the head (around Rnd 6) before drawing the yarn out through the starting point in the center of the face again. Repeat 2–3 times, pulling tightly to shape the cheeks.

Trunk

With A, make a 6-st AR.

Rnd 1: In bl, sc 6—6 sts.

Rnd 2: (Sc 2, sc 2 in next st) 2 times—8 sts.

Rnd 3: (Sc 1, sc 2 in next st, sc 2) 2 times—10 sts.

Rnd 4: Sc 10.

Rnd 5: (Sc 1, sc 2 in next st) 5 times—15 sts.

Fasten off, leaving a long tail for sewing.

Stuff trunk. With A, mattress stitch the open edge of the trunk to the center of the face between the eyes.

Tusks (make 2)

Starting with C, make a 4-st AR.

Rnd 1: In bl, sc 4—4 sts.

Rnd 2: (Sc 1, sc 2 in next st) 2 times—6 sts.

Cut C, change to A.

Rnd 3: Sc 2 in each st around—12 sts.

Rnd 4: Sc2tog 6 times—6 sts.

Fasten off, leaving a long tail for sewing.

Stuff tusks. With A, mattress stitch the open edges of the tusks to the face on either side of the trunk.

Ears (make 2)

With A, loosely ch 5.

Rnd 1: Working in back ridge loops, sc 3, sc 3 in next st. Rotate chain so front loops of chain are facing up. Starting in next st, sc 2, sc 2 in next st—10 sts.

Rnd 2: Sc 2 in next st, sc 2, sc 2 in next 3 sts, sc 2, sc 2 in next 2 sts—16 sts.

Rnd 3: Sc 2 in next st, sc 4, hdc 2 in next 4 sts, sc 4, sc 2 in next 3 sts—24 sts.

Fasten off, leaving a long tail for sewing.

With A, whipstitch the flat edges of the ears to the sides of the head, roughly 4–5 rnds behind the eyes with the hdc stitches oriented at the bottom of the ears.

Tail

Starting with A, make a 4-st AR.

Row 1: Sc 2 and turn, leaving remaining 2 sts unworked.

Rows 2–3: Ch 1, sc 2 and turn.

Fasten off A.

Tail Hair

Row 1: With B, (sl st 1, ch 1, sc 2) in 1st unworked st of tail. Sc 2 in next unworked st of tail and turn—4 sts.

Row 2: Ch 1, (sl st 1, ch 2, sl st) in next 4 sts and fasten off.

With A, sew the long edges of Rows 1–3 of the tail together. With B, sew only the ends of Row 1 of the tail hair section together. Attach the base of the tail to the back of the body.

Legs (make 4)

With A, make a 6-st AR.

Rnd 1: Sc 2 in each st around—12 sts.

Rnd 2: In bl, sc2tog 6 times—6 sts.

Fasten off, leaving a long tail for sewing.

Stuff and mattress stitch the open edges of the legs to the bottom of the body (around Rnds 12–13 for the front legs and Rnds 22–23 for the back legs) with about 8 sts of space between the inside edges of the legs.

NOTE: When sewing the legs to the bottom of the body, leave the yarn tails unsecured until all 4 legs are sewn in place to allow for easier removal and adjustments. Once you are satisfied with the leg placement, fasten off the yarn tails and weave in the ends.

FINISHING: Double a long piece of the bulky black yarn on a tapestry needle and embroider an eyebrow over each eye.

Weave in any remaining yarn tails.

Maxwell Monkey

Cheeky Maxwell Monkey is ready to have a swinging good time, provided there's a banana snack close by!

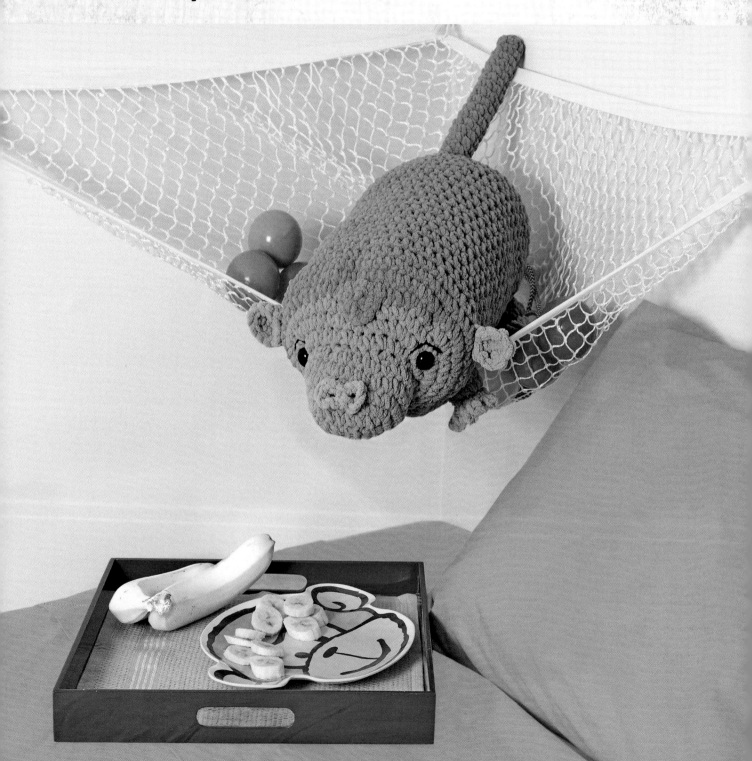

YARNS

Super Bulky Bernat® Blanket™ Yarn—
(A) #10801 Aquatic (180yds/165m)
(B) #10014 Sand (50yds/45m)

Bulky Berroco® Comfort® Chunky—
#5734 Liquorice (2yds/2m)

Optional (for child-safe eyes):
Worsted Berroco® Comfort®—#9734
Liquorice. See page 13 for pattern.

NOTIONS

- Size M/N (9.0mm) crochet hook
- Two 21mm black safety eyes
- Large steel tapestry needle
- Scissors
- Polyester fiberfill (12oz/340g)
- *Optional:* Large safety pins for place markers, bamboo straight pins

FINISHED SIZE

13" long, 9" wide, 7" tall

Maxwell Monkey

Body

Starting with B, loosely ch 8.

Rnd 1: Working in back ridge loops, sc 6, sc 3 in next st. Rotate chain so front loops of chain are facing up. Starting in next st, sc 5, sc 2 in next st—16 sts.

Rnd 2: Sc 2 in next st, sc 5, sc 2 in next 3 sts, sc 5, sc 2 in next 2 sts—22 sts.

Rnd 3: Sc 2 in next st, sc 7, sc 2 in next 4 sts, sc 7, sc 2 in next 3 sts—30 sts.

Rnd 4: Sc 2 in next 2 sts, sc 9, sc 2 in next 6 sts, sc 9, sc 2 in next 4 sts—42 sts.

Rnd 5: (Sc 3, sc 2 in next st, sc 3) 6 times—48 sts.

Cut B, change to A.

Rnd 6: (Sc 2, sc 2 in next st) 16 times—64 sts.

Rnds 7–8: Sc 64.

Rnd 9: (Sc 2, sc2tog) 16 times—48 sts.

Rnds 10–27: Sc 48.

Rnd 28: (Sc 2, sc2tog, sc 2) 8 times—40 sts.

Cut A, change to B.

Rnd 29: (Sc 3, sc2tog) 8 times—32 sts.

Rnd 30: (Sc 1, sc2tog, sc 1) 8 times—24 sts.

Rnd 31: Sc 1, sc2tog) 8 times—16 sts.

Fasten off, leaving a long tail for sewing. Stuff body firmly, but do not close hole.

If using plastic safety eyes, attach eyes to the front of the body between Rnds 3 and 4. You may wish to remove a bit of stuffing after positioning the eyes to make installing the eye backings easier. For children under 3, sew on crocheted eyes (page 13) or embroider eyes using the bulky black yarn and a tight grouping of satin stitches (page 10).

Using a mattress stitch, bring the edges of the hole in the back of the body together and sew the seam closed in a straight line level with the ch-8 at the beginning of your work.

Muzzle

With B, loosely ch 8.

Rnd 1: Working in back ridge loops, sc 6, sc 3 in next st. Rotate chain so front loops of chain are facing up. Starting in next st, sc 5, sc 2 in next st—16 sts.

Rnd 2: Sc 2 in next st, sc 5, sc 2 in next 3 sts, sc 5, sc 2 in next 2 sts—22 sts.

Rnd 3: Sc 2 in next st, sc 7, sc 2 in next 4 sts, sc 7, sc 2 in next 3 sts—30 sts.

Rnds 4–5: Sc 30.

Fasten off, leaving a long tail for sewing.

Line up the top edge of the muzzle between the eyes and the bottom edge of the muzzle across the lower edge of the face (around Rnd 5). Sew open edge down with mattress stitch, stuffing muzzle firmly before closing seam.

Forehead Peak

With A, loosely ch 3 and turn.

Row 1: Ch 1, sc 2 and turn—2 sts.

Row 2: Ch 1, sc2tog and pm—1 st.

Continue to sc evenly along the side, bottom edge, and opposite side of the peak until you reach the marker. (Sc 1, ch 1, sl st 1) in marked st, fasten off in next st and cut yarn, leaving a long tail for sewing.

Orient the point of the peak down toward the muzzle with the flat edge lined up with the color change rnd of the body (Rnd 6) and pin in place. With A, sew side edges down with a backstitch. Sew the top edge down using a mattress stitch.

Ears (make 2)

With B, make a 6-st AR.

Rnd 1: Sc 1, sc 2 in next st, hdc 2 in next 2 sts, sc 2 in next st, sc 1—10 sts.

Fasten off, leaving a long tail for sewing.

Using the leftover yarn tail, whipstitch the ears to the sides of the head, behind the eyes, between Rnds 7 and 8.

Nostrils

With B, loosely ch 10.

Row 1: Starting in 5th st from hook, sl st 1, sk to end of ch and sl st 1 to fasten off. The two loops will form the two nostrils. Cut yarn, leaving a long tail for sewing. Position the nostrils at the front of the muzzle and sew down with a series of small running stitches.

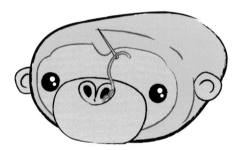

Belly

In B, loosely ch 8.

Rnd 1: Working in back ridge loops, sc 6, sc 3 in next st. Rotate chain so front loops of chain are facing up. Starting in next st, sc 5, sc 2 in next st—16 sts.

Rnd 2: Sc 2 in next st, sc 5, sc 2 in next 3 sts, sc 5, sc 2 in next 2 sts—22 sts.

Rnd 3: Sc 2 in next st, sc 7, sc 2 in next 4 sts, sc 7, sc 2 in next 3 sts—30 sts.

Rnd 4: Sc 2 in next 2 sts, sc 9, sc 2 in next 6 sts, sc 9, sc 2 in next 4 sts—42 sts.

Rnd 5: (Sc 3, sc 2 in next st, sc 3) 6 times—48 sts.

Rnd 6: (Sc 2, sc 2 in next st) 16 times—64 sts.

Fasten off, leaving a long tail for sewing.

Using a backstitch, sew the edge of the belly to the bottom of the body.

Tail

With A, make an 8-st AR.

Rnds 1–15: Sc 8, lightly stuff tail as you work.

Fasten off, leaving a long tail for sewing.

Sew the open edge of the tail to the back of the body, directly above the tan-colored patch.

Legs (make 4)

With A, make a 6-st AR.

Rnd 1: Sc 2 in each st around—12 sts.

Rnd 2: Sc2tog 6 times—6 sts.

Fasten off, leaving a long tail for sewing.

Stuff and mattress stitch the open edges of the legs to the bottom of the body (around Rnds 12–13 for the front legs and Rnds 22–23 for the back legs) with about 8 sts of space between the inside edges of the legs. The legs may overlap the belly slightly.

NOTE: When sewing the legs to the bottom of the body, leave the yarn tails unsecured until all 4 legs are sewn in place to allow for easier removal and adjustments. Once you are satisfied with the leg placement, fasten off the yarn tails and weave in the ends.

Feet (make 4)

With B, make an 8-st AR.

Rnd 1: Sl st 2, (sl st 1, ch 3, sl st in base st of ch-3) 4 times, sl st 2.

Fasten off, leaving a long tail for sewing.

With the toes pointing toward the front of the body, mattress stitch the tops of the feet to the bottoms of the legs.

FINISHING: Double a long piece of the bulky black yarn on a tapestry needle and embroider an eyebrow over each eye. Apply 2–3 short stitches inside the nostrils to darken them.

Weave in any remaining yarn tails.

Fern Fox

Clever Fern Fox loves a good mystery and is on the lookout for clues to her next adventure!

YARNS

Super Bulky Bernat® Blanket™ Yarn—
(A) #10630 Pumpkin Spice
(200yds/180m)
(B) #04008 Vanilla (50yds/45m)
(C) #10040 Coal (75yds/68m)

Bulky Berroco® Comfort®
Chunky—#5734 Liquorice (2yds/2m)

Optional (for child-safe eyes and nose):
Worsted Berroco® Comfort®—#9734
Liquorice. See page 13 for patterns.

NOTIONS

- Size M/N (9.0mm) crochet hook
- Two 21mm black safety eyes and one 29mm black triangle safety nose
- Large steel tapestry needle
- Scissors
- Polyester fiberfill (12oz/340g)
- Optional: Large safety pins for place markers, bamboo straight pins

FINISHED SIZE

13" long, 9" wide, 7" tall

Fern Fox

Body

With A, loosely ch 8.

Rnd 1: Working in back ridge loops, sc 6, sc 3 in next st. Rotate chain so front loops of chain are facing up. Starting in next st, sc 5, sc 2 in next st—16 sts.

Rnd 2: Sc 2 in next st, sc 5, sc 2 in next 3 sts, sc 5, sc 2 in next 2 sts—22 sts.

Rnd 3: Sc 2 in next st, sc 7, sc 2 in next 4 sts, sc 7, sc 2 in next 3 sts—30 sts.

Rnd 4: Sc 2 in next 2 sts, sc 9, sc 2 in next 6 sts, sc 9, sc 2 in next 4 sts—42 sts.

Rnd 5: (Sc 3, sc 2 in next st, sc 3) 6 times—48 sts.

Rnd 6: (Sc 2, sc 2 in next st) 16 times—64 sts.

Rnds 7–8: Sc 64.

Rnd 9: (Sc 2, sc2tog) 16 times—48 sts.

Rnds 10–27: Sc 48.

Rnd 28: (Sc 2, sc2tog, sc 2) 8 times—40 sts.

Rnd 29: (Sc 3, sc2tog) 8 times—32 sts.

Rnd 30: (Sc 1, sc2tog, sc 1) 8 times—24 sts.

Rnd 31: (Sc 1, sc2tog) 8 times—16 sts.

Fasten off, leaving a long tail for sewing. Stuff body firmly, but do not close hole.

If using plastic safety eyes, attach eyes to the front of the body between Rnds 3 and 4. You may wish to remove a bit of stuffing after positioning the eyes to make installing the eye backings easier. For children under 3, sew on crocheted eyes (page 13) or embroider eyes using the bulky black yarn and a tight grouping of satin stitches (page 10).

Using a mattress stitch, bring the edges of the hole in the back of the body together and sew the seam closed in a straight line level with the ch-8 at the beginning of your work.

Refer to Changing Colors on page 7 for tips on how to make smoother color changes!

Muzzle, Cheeks, and Chin

Starting with B, make an 8-st AR.

Change to A.

Rnd 1: Sc 2 in next 2 sts; change to B, sc 2 in next 4 sts; change to A, sc 2 in next 2 sts—16 sts.

Rnd 2: Sc 2, sc2tog; change to B, sc2tog, pm, sc 4, sc2tog; change to A, sc2tog, sc 2—12 sts.

Cut both A and B and fasten off.

CHEEKS AND CHIN

Row 1: To rejoin B, (sl st 1, ch 1, sc 1) in marked st (counts as 1st sc). Continue working in B sts only, sc 2 in next 4 sts, sc 1, turn—10 sts.

Row 2: Ch 2, hdc 1, hdc 2 in next st, sc 1, sc 2 in next 4 sts, sc 1, hdc 2 in next st, hdc 1, turn—16 sts.

Row 3: Ch 1, sc 2 in next 3 sts, sc 10, sc 2 in next 3 sts, turn—22 sts.

Row 4: Ch 1, sc2tog, sc 18, sc2tog, turn—20 sts.

Row 5: Ch 1, (sl st 1, ch 3. Starting in 2nd ch from hook, sl st 2, sl st 1 in next st) 3 times. Sc 8 (sl st 1 in next st, sl st 1, ch 3. Starting in 2nd ch from hook, sl st 2) 3 times.

Continue to sc along the top edge of the cheek until you reach the "A" edge of the muzzle. Change to A and sl st along the back edge of the "A" edge of the muzzle until you reach the opposite cheek. Cut A. Float B across back of work. With B, sc along top edge of the opposite cheek until you reach the 1st stitch of Row 5 and fasten off.

If using a plastic safety nose, attach safety nose in the front of the muzzle where the A and B halves meet.

Attach open edge of muzzle to the front of the body with a mattress stitch. Add a small amount of stuffing to only the muzzle before closing the seam. For children under 3, sew on crocheted nose (page 13) or embroider nose using the bulky black yarn and a tight grouping of satin stitches (page 10) after you have attached the muzzle to the front of the face.

Flatten the cheeks and the chin down to the front of the body, leaving the whisker fringe loose. Backstitch cheeks and chin edges down using B and a tapestry needle.

With B, draw a long stitch out from below the muzzle in the center of the face and into the bottom of the head just below the bottom edge of the "B" chin before drawing the yarn out through the starting point below the muzzle again. Repeat 2–3 times, pulling tightly to shape the cheeks.

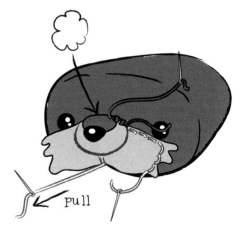

Belly

With B, loosely ch 8.

Rnd 1: Working in back ridge loops, sc 6, sc 3 in next st. Rotate chain so front loops of chain are facing up. Starting in next st, sc 5, sc 2 in next st—16 sts.

Rnd 2: Sc 2 in next st, sc 5, sc 2 in next 3 sts, sc 5, sc 2 in next 2 sts—22 sts.

Rnd 3: Sc 2 in next st, sc 7, sc 2 in next 4 sts, sc 7, sc 2 in next 3 sts—30 sts.

Rnd 4: Sc 2 in next 2 sts, sc 9, sc 2 in next 6 sts, sc 9, sc 2 in next 4 sts—42 sts.

Rnd 5: (Sc 3, sc 2 in next st, sc 3) 6 times—48 sts.

Rnd 6: (Sc 2, sc 2 in next st) 16 times—64 sts.

Fasten off, leaving a long tail for sewing.

Using a backstitch, sew the edge of the belly to the bottom of the body.

Tail

Starting with B, make a 4-st AR.

Rnd 1: Sc 2 in each st around—8 sts.

Rnd 2: Sc 2 in each st around—16 sts.

Rnd 3: Sc 16.

Cut B, change to A.

Rnd 4: (Sc 6, sc2tog) 2 times—14 sts.

Rnd 5: (Sc 5, sc2tog) 2 times—12 sts.

Rnd 6: (Sc 4, sc2tog) 2 times—10 sts.

Rnd 7: (Sc 3, sc2tog) 2 times—8 sts.

Rnd 8: (Sc 2, sc2tog) 2 times—6 sts.

Rnds 9–10: Sc 6.

Fasten off, leaving a long tail for sewing.

Stuff tail. Using a mattress stitch, sew open edge of tail to back of body.

Outer Ears (make 2)

With C, loosely ch 4.

Row 1: Starting in 2nd ch from hook, sc 3 and turn—3 sts.

Row 2: Ch 1, sc 1, sk 1, sc 1 and turn—2 sts.

Row 3: Ch 1, sc2tog and pm—1 st.

Continue to sc evenly along the side, bottom edge, and opposite side of the ear until you reach the marker. (Sc 1, ch 2, sl st 1) in marked st, fasten off in next st and cut yarn, leaving a long tail for sewing.

Inner Ears (make 2)

With B, loosely ch 3.

Row 1: Ch 1, sc 2 and turn—2 sts.

Row 2: Ch 1, sc2tog and pm—1 st.

Continue to sc evenly along the side, bottom edge, and opposite side of the ear until you reach the marker. (Sc 1, ch 2, sl st 1) in marked st, fasten off in next st and cut yarn, leaving a long tail for sewing.

Sew the inner ear to the surface of the outer ear. Whipstitch the flat edge of the ears to the head 4–5 rnds behind the eyes.

Legs (make 4)

Starting with C, make a 6-st AR.

Rnd 1: Sc 2 in each st around—12 sts.

Cut C, change to A.

Rnd 2: Sc2tog 6 times—6 sts.

Rnd 3: Sc 6.

Fasten off, leaving a long tail for sewing.

Stuff and mattress stitch the open edges of the legs to the bottom of the body (around Rnds 12–13 for the front legs and Rnds 22–23 for the back legs) with about 8 sts of space between the inside edges of the legs. The legs may overlap the belly slightly.

NOTE: When sewing the legs to the bottom of the body, leave the yarn tails unsecured until all 4 legs are sewn in place to allow for easier removal and adjustments. Once you are satisfied with the leg placement, fasten off the yarn tails and weave in the ends.

FINISHING: Double a long piece of the bulky black yarn on a tapestry needle and embroider an eyebrow over each eye.

Weave in any remaining yarn tails.

Bobby Beaver

Bobby Beaver would be happy to hang out at home with you.
Just keep him away from your wooden furniture.

YARNS

Super Bulky Bernat® Blanket™ Yarn—
(A) #10430 Purple Plum (200yds/185m)
(B) #10029 Taupe (50yds/45m)
(C) #04008 Vanilla (2yds/2m)

Bulky Berroco® Comfort®
Chunky—#5734 Liquorice (2yds/2m)

Optional (for child-safe eyes and nose):
Worsted Berroco® Comfort®—#9734
Liquorice. See page 13 for patterns.

NOTIONS

- Size M/N (9.0mm) crochet hook
- Two 21mm black safety eyes and one 29mm black triangle safety nose
- Large steel tapestry needle
- Scissors
- Polyester fiberfill (12oz/340g)
- Optional: Large safety pins for place markers, bamboo straight pins

FINISHED SIZE

13" long, 9" wide, 7" tall

Bobby Beaver

Body

With A, loosely ch 8.

Rnd 1: Working in back ridge loops, sc 6, sc 3 in next st. Rotate chain so front loops of chain are facing up. Starting in next st, sc 5, sc 2 in next st—16 sts.

Rnd 2: Sc 2 in next st, sc 5, sc 2 in next 3 sts, sc 5, sc 2 in next 2 sts—22 sts.

Rnd 3: Sc 2 in next st, sc 7, sc 2 in next 4 sts, sc 7, sc 2 in next 3 sts—30 sts.

Rnd 4: Sc 2 in next 2 sts, sc 9, sc 2 in next 6 sts, sc 9, sc 2 in next 4 sts—42 sts.

Rnd 5: (Sc 3, sc 2 in next st, sc 3) 6 times—48 sts.

Rnd 6: (Sc 2, sc 2 in next st) 16 times—64 sts.

Rnds 7–8: Sc 64.

Rnd 9: (Sc 2, sc2tog) 16 times—48 sts.

Rnds 10–27: Sc 48.

Rnd 28: (Sc 2, sc2tog, sc 2) 8 times—40 sts.

Rnd 29: (Sc 3, sc2tog) 8 times—32 sts.

Rnd 30: (Sc 1, sc2tog, sc 1) 8 times—24 sts.

Rnd 31: (Sc 1, sc2tog) 8 times—16 sts.

Fasten off, leaving a long tail for sewing. Stuff body firmly, but do not close hole.

If using plastic safety eyes, attach eyes to the front of the body between Rnds 3 and 4. You may wish to remove a bit of stuffing after positioning the eyes to make installing the eye backings easier. For children under 3, sew on crocheted eyes (page 13) or embroider eyes using the bulky black yarn and a tight grouping of satin stitches (page 10).

Using a mattress stitch, bring the edges of the hole in the back of the body together and sew the seam closed in a straight line level with the ch-8 at the beginning of your work.

Muzzle

With A, make a 7-st AR.

Rnd 1: Sc 2 in each st around—14 sts.

Rnd 2: (Sc 3, hdc 2 in next 4 sts) 2 times—22 sts.

Rnds 3–4: Sc 22.

Fasten off, leaving a long tail for sewing.

With the hdc increases oriented on the left and right sides of the muzzle, attach safety nose between Rnds 1 and 2 directly above the center of the muzzle.

Attach open edge of muzzle to the front of the body with a mattress stitch and stuff before closing seam. For children under 3, sew on crocheted nose (page 13) or embroider nose using the bulky black yarn and a tight grouping of satin stitches (page 10) after you have attached the muzzle to the front of the face.

To add a lip cleft below a plastic safety nose, tie the middle of an 18–20" strand of the bulky black yarn around the post of the nose. Thread your tapestry needle with the yarn tails and draw a long stitch down over the front of the muzzle, and fasten off beneath the muzzle to create the lip cleft detail.

NOTE: The same long stitch can also be embroidered onto the muzzle when using child-safe nose options (page 13).

Tooth

With C, make a 5-st AR but do not join. Cut yarn and pull through loop on hook to fasten off.

Sew flat edge of semicircle-shaped tooth to the underside of the muzzle.

Ears (make 2)

With A, make a 6-st AR but do not join. Cut yarn and pull through loop on hook to fasten off.

With A, whipstitch flat edge of semicircle-shaped ears 4 rnds behind the eyes.

Legs (make 4)

With A, make a 6-st AR.

Rnd 1: Sc 2 in each st around—12 sts.

Rnd 2: Sc2tog 6 times—6 sts.

Fasten off, leaving a long tail for sewing.

Stuff and mattress stitch the open edges of the legs to the bottom of the body (around Rnds 12–13 for the front legs and Rnds 22–23 for the back legs) with about 8 sts of space between the inside edges of the legs.

NOTE: When sewing the legs to the bottom of the body, leave the yarn tails unsecured until all 4 legs are sewn in place to allow for easier removal and adjustments. Once you are satisfied with the leg placement, fasten off the yarn tails and weave in the ends.

Feet (make 4)

With B, make an 8-st AR.

Rnd 1: Sl st 2, (sl st 1, ch 3, sl st 1) in next 4 sts, sl st 2.

Fasten off, leaving a long tail for sewing.

With the toes pointing toward the front of the body, mattress stitch the tops of the feet to the bottoms of the legs.

Tail

With B, make an 8-st AR.

Rnd 1: Sc 1 in each st around—16 sts.

Rnd 2: (Sc 3, sc 2 in next st) 4 times—20 sts.

Rnds 3–4: Sc 20.

Rnd 5: (Sc 4, sc 2 in next st) 4 times—24 sts.

Rnds 6–8: Sc 24.

Rnd 9: (Sc 4, sc2tog) 4 times—20 sts.

Rnd 10: (Sc 3, sc2tog) 4 times—16 sts.

Rnd 11: (Sc 2, sc2tog) 4 times—12 sts.

Rnds 12–13: Sc 12.

Fasten off, leaving a long tail for sewing.

Flatten opening and whipstitch seam closed using leftover yarn tail.

Whipstitch the seamed edge of the tail to the back of the body.

FINISHING: Weave in any remaining yarn tails.

Olive Owl

Olive, the fluffy and feathery owl,
knows that reading every day is a wise habit!

YARNS

Super Bulky Bernat® Blanket™ Yarn—
(A) #10029 Taupe (200yds/180m)
(B) #04008 Vanilla (50yds/45m)
(C) #10014 Sand (25yds/22m)
(D) #12003 School Bus Yellow (5yds/5m)

Optional (for embroidered eyes):
Bulky Berroco® Comfort®
Chunky—#5734 Liquorice (2yds/2m)

Optional (for child-safe eyes): Worsted
Berroco® Comfort®—#9734 Liquorice.
See page 13 for pattern.

NOTIONS

• Size M/N (9.0mm) crochet hook
• Two 21mm black safety eyes
• Large steel tapestry needle
• Scissors
• Polyester fiberfill (12oz/340g)
• *Optional*: Large safety pins for place markers, bamboo straight pins

FINISHED SIZE

13" long, 9" wide, 7" tall

Olive Owl

Body

Starting with B, loosely ch 8.

Rnd 1: Working in back ridge loops, sc 6, sc 3 in next st. Rotate chain so front loops of chain are facing up. Starting in next st, sc 5, sc 2 in next st—16 sts.

Rnd 2: Sc 2 in next st, sc 5, sc 2 in next 3 sts, sc 5, sc 2 in next 2 sts—22 sts.

Rnd 3: Sc 2 in next st, sc 7, sc 2 in next 4 sts, sc 7, sc 2 in next 3 sts—30 sts.

Rnd 4: Sc 2 in next 2 sts, sc 9, sc 2 in next 6 sts, sc 9, sc 2 in next 4 sts—42 sts.

Rnd 5: (Sc 3, sc 2 in next st, sc 3) 6 times—48 sts.

Cut B, change to A.

Rnd 6: (Sc 2, sc 2 in next st) 16 times—64 sts.

Rnds 7–8: Sc 64.

Rnd 9: (Sc 2, sc2tog) 16 times—48 sts.

Rnds 10–27: Sc 48.

Rnd 28: (Sc 2, sc2tog, sc 2) 8 times—40 sts.

Rnd 29: (Sc 3, sc2tog) 8 times—32 sts.

Rnd 30: (Sc 1, sc2tog, sc 1) 8 times—24 sts.

Rnd 31: (Sc 1, sc2tog) 8 times—16 sts.

Fasten off, leaving a long tail for sewing. Stuff body firmly.

Using a mattress stitch, bring the edges of the hole in the back of the body together and sew the seam closed in a straight line level with the ch-8 at the beginning of your work.

With B, draw a long stitch out from below the muzzle in the center of the face and into the bottom edge of the face (around Rnd 5) before drawing the yarn out through the starting point in the center of the face again. Repeat 2–3 times, pulling tightly to shape the cheeks.

For children under 3, sew on crocheted eyes (page 13) or embroider eyes using the bulky black yarn and a tight grouping of satin stitches (page 10) to the center of the eye spots.

With C, backstitch the eye ruffles down so that the eyes sit roughly between Rnds 3 and 4 on either side of the beak and the ruffles are positioned along the outer edges.

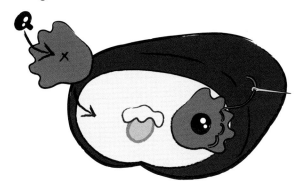

Beak

With D, make a 6-st AR.

Rnds 1–2: Sc 6.

Fasten off, leaving a long tail for sewing.

Stuff beak and sew open edge to middle of face.

Beak Ruffle

With B, make a 4-st AR but do not join. Turn and work semicircle shape in rows.

Row 1: (sl st 1, ch 2, sl st 1) in next 4 sts.

Fasten off, leaving a long tail for sewing.

Whipstitch beak ruffle to the face directly above the beak.

Eye Ruffles (make 2)

With C, make an 8-st AR.

Rnd 1: Sc 2 in each st around—16 sts.

Rnd 2: (Sl st 1, ch 3, sl st 1) 5 times, sl st 6.

Fasten off, leaving a long tail for sewing.

If using plastic safety eyes, insert the eye posts into the middle of the eye ruffles and secure the backings.

Forehead Peak

With A, loosely ch 3 and turn.

Row 1: Ch 1, sc 2 and turn—2 sts.

Row 2: Ch 1, sc2tog and pm—1 st.

Continue to sc evenly along the side, bottom edge, and opposite side of the peak until you reach the marker. (Sc 1, ch 1, sl st 1) in marked st, fasten off in next st and cut yarn, leaving a long tail for sewing.

Orient the point of the peak down toward the beak with the flat edge lined up with the color change rnd of the body (Rnd 6) and pin in place. With A, sew side edges down with a backstitch. Sew the top edge down using a mattress stitch.

Ear Feathers (make 2)

With A, make a 3-st AR but do not join. Turn and work semicircle shape in rows.

Row 1: (Sl st 1, ch 3, sl st 1) in next 3 sts.

Fasten off, leaving a long tail for sewing.

With A, whipstitch flat edge of ear feathers to side of head (between Rnds 8 and 9) directly behind the eyes.

Belly

In B, loosely ch 8.

Rnd 1: Working in back ridge loops, sc 6, sc 3 in next st. Rotate chain so front loops of chain are facing up. Starting in next st, sc 5, sc 2 in next st—16 sts.

Rnd 2: Sc 2 in next st, sc 5, sc 2 in next 3 sts, sc 5, sc 2 in next 2 sts—22 sts.

Rnd 3: Sc 2 in next st, sc 7, sc 2 in next 4 sts, sc 7, sc 2 in next 3 sts—30 sts.

Rnd 4: Sc 2 in next 2 sts, sc 9, sc 2 in next 6 sts, sc 9, sc 2 in next 4 sts—42 sts.

Rnd 5: (Sc 3, sc 2 in next st, sc 3) 6 times—48 sts.

Rnd 6: (Sc 2, sc 2 in next st) 16 times—64 sts.

Fasten off, leaving a long tail for sewing.

Using a backstitch, sew the edge of the belly to the bottom of the body.

Wings and Tail (make 3)

With A, make an 8-st AR, but do not join. Turn and work semicircle shape in rows.

Row 1: Ch 1, sl st 2, sc 2 in next 4 sts, sl st 2 and turn—12 sts.

Row 2: Ch 1, sl st 2, (sl st 1, ch 2, sl st 1) in next 8 sts, sl st 2.

Fasten off, leaving a long tail for sewing.

Sew straight edges of the wings to the sides of the body so the ruffled edges stick out.

For the tail, pinch the corners of Row 2 together and secure in place with a few stitches. The tail will form a cupped shape. Sew the pinched base of the tail to the back of the body with the cupped side facing out.

Feet (make 2)

With D, make a 7-st AR.

Rnd 1: Sl st 2, (sl st 1, ch 3, sl st 1) in next 3 sts, sl st 2.

Fasten off, leaving a long tail for sewing.

With the toes pointing toward the front of the body, mattress stitch the tops of the feet to the bottom of the body (around Rnds 22–23) with about 8 sts of space between the inside edges.

FINISHING: Weave in any remaining yarn tails.

Braden Bear

Braden Bear is looking for any excuse to hibernate in comfort and would be delighted to share your cozy tent and sleeping bag.

YARNS

Super Bulky Bernat® Blanket™ Yarn—
(A) #04744 Overcast (200yds/185m)
(B) #04008 Vanilla (50yds/45m)

Bulky Berroco® Comfort®
Chunky—#5734 Liquorice (2yds/2m)

Optional (for child-safe eyes and nose):
Worsted Berroco® Comfort®—#9734
Liquorice. See page 13 for patterns.

NOTIONS

- Size M/N (9.0mm) crochet hook
- Two 21mm black safety eyes and one 29mm black triangle safety nose
- Large steel tapestry needle
- Scissors
- Polyester fiberfill (12oz/340g)
- *Optional*: Large safety pins for place markers, bamboo straight pins

FINISHED SIZE
13" long, 9" wide, 7" tall

Braden Bear

Body

With A, loosely ch 8.

Rnd 1: Working in back ridge loops, sc 6, sc 3 in next st. Rotate chain so front loops of chain are facing up. Starting in next st, sc 5, sc 2 in next st—16 sts.

Rnd 2: Sc 2 in next st, sc 5, sc 2 in next 3 sts, sc 5, sc 2 in next 2 sts—22 sts.

Rnd 3: Sc 2 in next st, sc 7, sc 2 in next 4 sts, sc 7, sc 2 in next 3 sts—30 sts.

Rnd 4: Sc 2 in next 2 sts, sc 9, sc 2 in next 6 sts, sc 9, sc 2 in next 4 sts—42 sts.

Rnd 5: (Sc 3, sc 2 in next st, sc 3) 6 times—48 sts.

Rnd 6: (Sc 2, sc 2 in next st) 16 times—64 sts.

Rnds 7–8: Sc 64.

Rnd 9: (Sc 2, sc2tog) 16 times—48 sts.

Rnds 10–27: Sc 48.

Rnd 28: (Sc 2, sc2tog, sc 2) 8 times—40 sts.

Rnd 29: (Sc 3, sc2tog) 8 times—32 sts.

Rnd 30: (Sc 1, sc2tog, sc 1) 8 times—24 sts.

Rnd 31: (Sc 1, sc2tog) 8 times—16 sts.

Fasten off, leaving a long tail for sewing. Stuff body firmly, but do not close hole.

If using plastic safety eyes, attach eyes to the front of the body between Rnds 3 and 4. You may wish to remove a bit of stuffing after positioning the eyes to make installing the eye backings easier. For children under 3, sew on crocheted eyes (page 13) or embroider eyes using the bulky black yarn and a tight grouping of satin stitches (page 10).

Using a mattress stitch, bring the edges of the hole in the back of the body together and sew the seam closed in a straight line level with the ch-8 at the beginning of your work.

Muzzle

With B, make a 7-st AR.

Rnd 1: Sc 2 in each st around—14 sts.

Rnd 2: (Sl st 3, hdc 2 in next 4 sts) 2 times—22 sts.

Fasten off, leaving a long tail for sewing.

With the hdc increases oriented on the left and right sides of the muzzle, attach safety nose between Rnds 1 and 2 directly above the center of the muzzle.

Attach open edge of muzzle to the front of the body with a mattress stitch and stuff before closing seam. For children under 3, sew on crocheted nose (page 13) or embroider nose using the bulky black yarn and a tight grouping of satin stitches (page 10) after you have attached the muzzle to the front of the face.

Belly

With B, loosely ch 8.

Rnd 1: Working in back ridge loops, sc 6, sc 3 in next st. Rotate chain so front loops of chain are facing up. Starting in next st, sc 5, sc 2 in next st—16 sts.

Rnd 2: Sc 2 in next st, sc 5, sc 2 in next 3 sts, sc 5, sc 2 in next 2 sts—22 sts.

Rnd 3: Sc 2 in next st, sc 7, sc 2 in next 4 sts, sc 7, sc 2 in next 3 sts—30 sts.

Rnd 4: Sc 2 in next 2 sts, sc 9, sc 2 in next 6 sts, sc 9, sc 2 in next 4 sts—42 sts.

Rnd 5: (Sc 3, sc 2 in next st, sc 3) 6 times—48 sts.

Rnd 6: (Sc 2, sc 2 in next st) 16 times—64 sts.

Fasten off, leaving a long tail for sewing.

Using a backstitch, sew the edge of the belly to the bottom of the body.

Ears (make 2)

With A, make a 6-st AR but do not join. Turn and work semicircle shape in rows.

Row 1: Ch 1, sc 1 in each st to end—6 sts.

Sl st into ch 1 at beg of Row 1 to pinch bottom of ear together. Fasten off.

Whipstitch the pinched end of the ear to the head 4 to 5 rnds above the eye spots.

Tail

With A, make a 4-st AR.

Rnd 1: Sc 2 in each st around—8 sts.

Rnd 2: Sc 8.

Fasten off, leaving a long tail for sewing.

Stuff tail and sew open edge to back of body using a mattress stitch.

Legs (make 4)

With A, make a 6-st AR.

Rnd 1: Sc 2 in each st around—12 sts.

Rnd 2: Sc2tog 6 times—6 sts.

Fasten off, leaving a long tail for sewing.

Stuff and mattress stitch the open edges of the legs to the bottom of the body (around Rnds 12–13 for the front legs and Rnds 22–23 for the back legs) with about 8 sts of space between the inside edges of the legs. The legs may overlap the belly slightly.

NOTE: When sewing the legs to the bottom of the body, leave the yarn tails unsecured until all 4 legs are sewn in place to allow for easier removal and adjustments. Once you are satisfied with the leg placement, fasten off the yarn tails and weave in the ends.

FINISHING: Double up a long piece of the bulky black yarn on a tapestry needle and embroider an eyebrow over each eye. Weave in any remaining yarn tails.

Wally Whale

With a flip of his tail and a spritz of his spout,
adorable Wally Whale is ready to have a swimmingly good time!

YARNS

Super Bulky Bernat® Blanket™ Yarn—
(A) #04734 Baby Teal (200yds/180m)
(B) #04005 White (120yds/110m)

Bulky Berroco® Comfort®
Chunky—#5734 Liquorice (2yds/2m)

Optional (for child-safe eyes):
Worsted Berroco® Comfort®—#9734
Liquorice. See page 13 for pattern.

NOTIONS

- Size M/N (9.0mm) crochet hook
- Two 21mm black safety eyes
- Large steel tapestry needle
- Scissors
- Polyester fiberfill (12oz/340g)
- *Optional:* Large safety pins for place markers, bamboo straight pins

FINISHED SIZE

13" long, 9" wide, 7" tall

Wally Whale

Body

With A, loosely ch 8.

Rnd 1: Working in back ridge loops, sc 6, sc 3 in next st. Rotate chain so front loops of chain are facing up. Starting in next st, sc 5, sc 2 in next st—16 sts.

Rnd 2: Sc 2 in next st, sc 5, sc 2 in next 3 sts, sc 5, sc 2 in next 2 sts—22 sts.

Rnd 3: Sc 2 in next st, sc 7, sc 2 in next 4 sts, sc 7, sc 2 in next 3 sts—30 sts.

Rnd 4: Sc 2 in next 2 sts, sc 9, sc 2 in next 6 sts, sc 9, sc 2 in next 4 sts—42 sts.

Rnd 5: (Sc 3, sc 2 in next st, sc 3) 6 times—48 sts.

Rnd 6: (Sc 2, sc 2 in next st) 16 times—64 sts.

Rnds 7–8: Sc 64.

Rnd 9: (Sc 2, sc2tog) 16 times—48 sts.

Rnds 10–27: Sc 48.

Rnd 28: (Sc 2, sc2tog, sc 2) 8 times—40 sts.

Rnd 29: (Sc 3, sc2tog) 8 times—32 sts.

Rnd 30: (Sc 1, sc2tog, sc 1) 8 times—24 sts.

Rnd 31: (Sc 1, sc2tog) 8 times—16 sts.

Fasten off, leaving a long tail for sewing. Stuff body firmly, but do not close hole.

If using plastic safety eyes, attach eyes to the front of the body between Rnds 5 and 6. You may wish to remove a bit of stuffing after positioning the eyes to make installing the eye backings easier. For children under 3, sew on crocheted eyes (page 13) or embroider eyes using the bulky black yarn and a tight grouping of satin stitches (page 10).

Using a mattress stitch, bring the edges of the hole in the back of the body together and sew the seam closed in a straight line level with the ch-8 at the beginning of your work.

Belly

With B, loosely ch 25.

Row 1: Starting in 2nd ch from hook, sc 23, sc 2 in next st and turn—25 sts.

Row 2: Ch 1, sl st 25 and turn.

Row 3: Ch 1, sc 24, sc 2 in next st and turn—26 sts.

Row 4: Ch 1, sl st 26 and turn.

Row 5: Ch 1, sc 25, sc 2 in next st and turn—27 sts.

Row 6: Ch 1, sl st 27 and turn.

Row 7: Ch 1, sc 26, sc 2 in next st and turn—28 sts.

Row 8: Ch 1, sl st 28 and turn.

Row 9: Ch 1, sc 27, sc 2 in next st and turn—29 sts.

Row 10: Ch 1, sl st 29 and turn.

Row 11: Ch 1, sc 29 and turn—29 sts.

Repeat Rows 10–11 one more time.

Row 14: Ch 1, sl st 29 and turn.

Row 15: Ch 1, sc 27, sc2tog and turn—28 sts.

Row 16: Ch 1, sl st 28 and turn.

Row 17: Ch 1, sc 26, sc2tog and turn—27 sts.

Row 18: Ch 1, sl st 27 and turn.

Row 19: Ch 1, sc 25, sc2tog and turn—26 sts.

Row 20: Ch 1, sl st 26 and turn.

Row 21: Ch 1, sc 24, sc2tog and turn—25 sts.

Row 22: Ch 1, sl st 25 and turn.

Sc along bottom edge of work, sl st along ch-25 edge of work, and sc along top edge of work until you reach the beginning of Row 22.

Fasten off, leaving a long tail for sewing.

Place and pin the curved front edge of the belly to the middle of the face so the center of the curve sits between the eyes. Pin the remaining belly edges down evenly to the underside of the body. Sew edge in place with a backstitch.

Tail

With A, loosely ch 12.

Rnd 1: Working in back ridge loops, sc 10, sc 3 in next st. Rotate chain so front loops of chain are facing up. Starting in next st, sc 9, sc 2 in next st—24 sts.

Rnd 2: Sc 2 in next st, sc 9, sc 2 in next 3 sts, sc 9, sc 2 in next 2 sts—30 sts.

Rnds 3–4: Sc 30.

Stuff tail. Flatten open edge to line up stitches. Working through both edges at the same time, sc to end of row to close the seam.

With A yarn on tapestry needle, attach the yarn in the middle of Rnd 1 at the base of the tail. Working from front to back, loop yarn over the top of the tail and back to starting point at the tail base. Repeat 1–2 more times, pulling tightly to cinch down the middle of the tail to create the two sides of the fin. Fasten off yarn to secure.

Whipstitch the bottom edge of the tail to the top of the whale's back.

Side Fins (make 2)

With A, make a 6-st AR.

Rnd 1: Sc 1, sc 2 in next st, hdc 2 in next 2 sts, sc 2 in next st, sc 1—10 sts.

Fasten off, leaving a long tail for sewing.

There will be a slight taper to Rnd 1 of the side fins where the rnd starts and ends with a sc st. Whipstitch the tapered ends of the side fins just above the edge of the belly, 8 rnds behind the eyes.

Spout

Starting with A, make an 8-st AR. Do not pull adjustable ring closed all the way.

Rnd 1: In bl, sc 8.

Cut A, change to B.

Rnd 2: In bl, (sc 1, sc 2 in next st) 4 times—12 sts.

Rnd 3: (Sl st 1, [sl st 1, ch 3, sl st 1] in next st) 6 times—18 sts.

Fasten off, leaving a long tail for sewing.

Draw "B" Rnds 2 and 3 up and out through the opening in the middle of the adjustable ring (effectively turning the spout partially inside out). Once the white portion of the spout has been drawn out through the center of the 8-st AR, pull beginning yarn tail to tighten the ring (take care not to pull the yarn too hard as it can have a tendency to break). Sew the blue portion of the spout to the top of the whale's body slightly in front of the side fins.

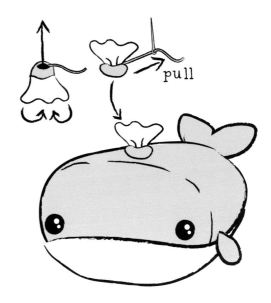

FINISHING: Double a long piece of the bulky black yarn on a tapestry needle and embroider an eyebrow over each eye.

Weave in any remaining yarn tails.

Sharon Shark

Don't let the toothy grin scare you off; soft and smiley Sharon Shark just wants to jam out to her favorite shark-themed tunes with you.

YARNS

Super Bulky Bernat® Blanket™ Yarn—
(A) #10046 Pale Grey (200yds/180m)
(B) #04005 White (100yds/91m)

Bulky Berroco® Comfort®
Chunky—#5734 Liquorice (2yds/2m)

Optional (for child-safe eyes):
Worsted Berroco® Comfort®—#9734
Liquorice. See page 13 for pattern.

NOTIONS

- Size M/N (9.0mm) crochet hook
- Two 21mm black safety eyes
- Large steel tapestry needle
- Scissors
- Polyester fiberfill (12oz/340g)
- *Optional:* Large safety pins for place markers, bamboo straight pins

FINISHED SIZE

13" long, 9" wide, 7" tall

Sharon Shark

Body

With A, loosely ch 8.

Rnd 1: Working in back ridge loops, sc 6, sc 3 in next st. Rotate chain so front loops of chain are facing up. Starting in next st, sc 5, sc 2 in next st—16 sts.

Rnd 2: Sc 2 in next st, sc 5, sc 2 in next 3 sts, sc 5, sc 2 in next 2 sts—22 sts.

Rnd 3: Sc 2 in next st, sc 7, sc 2 in next 4 sts, sc 7, sc 2 in next 3 sts—30 sts.

Rnd 4: Sc 2 in next 2 sts, sc 9, sc 2 in next 6 sts, sc 9, sc 2 in next 4 sts—42 sts.

Rnd 5: (Sc 3, sc 2 in next st, sc 3) 6 times—48 sts.

Rnd 6: (Sc 2, sc 2 in next st) 16 times—64 sts.

Rnds 7–8: Sc 64.

Rnd 9: (Sc 2, sc2tog) 16 times—48 sts.

Rnds 10–27: Sc 48.

Rnd 28: (Sc 2, sc2tog, sc 2) 8 times—40 sts.

Rnd 29: (Sc 3, sc2tog) 8 times—32 sts.

Rnd 30: (Sc 1, sc2tog, sc 1) 8 times—24 sts.

Rnd 31: (Sc 1, sc2tog) 8 times—16 sts.

Fasten off, leaving a long tail for sewing. Stuff body firmly, but do not close hole.

If using plastic safety eyes, attach eyes to the front of the body between Rnds 5 and 6. You may wish to remove a bit of stuffing after positioning the eyes to make installing the eye backings easier. For children under 3, sew on crocheted eyes (page 13) or embroider eyes using the bulky black yarn and a tight grouping of satin stitches (page 10).

Using a mattress stitch, bring the edges of the hole in the back of the body together and sew the seam closed in a straight line level with the ch-8 at the beginning of your work.

Belly

With B, loosely ch 25.

Row 1: Starting in 2nd ch from hook, sc 23, sc 2 in next st and turn—25 sts.

Row 2: Ch 1, sc 25 and turn.

Row 3: Ch 1, sc 24, sc 2 in next st and turn—26 sts.

Row 4: Ch 1, sc 26 and turn.

Row 5: Ch 1, sc 25, sc 2 in next st and turn—27 sts.

Row 6: Ch 1, sc 27 and turn.

Row 7: Ch 1, sc 26, sc 2 in next st and turn—28 sts.

Row 8: Ch 1, sc 28 and turn.

Row 9: Ch 1, sc 27, sc 2 in next st and turn—29 sts.

Rows 10–14: Ch 1, sc 29 and turn.

Row 15: Ch 1, sc 27, sc2tog and turn—28 sts.

Row 16: Ch 1, sc 28 and turn.

Row 17: Ch 1, sc 26, sc2tog and turn—27 sts.

Row 18: Ch 1, sc 27 and turn.

Row 19: Ch 1, sc 25, sc2tog and turn—26 sts.

Row 20: Ch 1, sc 26 and turn.

Row 21: Ch 1, sc 24, sc2tog and turn—25 sts.

Row 22: Ch 1, sc 25 and turn.

Sc along bottom edge of work, sl st along ch-25 edge of work, and sc along top edge of work until you reach the beginning of Row 22.

Fasten off, leaving a long tail for sewing.

Place and pin the curved front edge of the belly to the middle of the face so the center of the curve sits just below the eyes. Pin the remaining belly edges down evenly to the underside of the body. Sew edge in place with a backstitch.

Dorsal Fin

With A, loosely ch 10.

Rnd 1: Working in back ridge loops, sc 8, sc 3 in next st. Rotate chain so front loops of chain are facing up. Starting in next st, sc 7, sc 2 in next st—20 sts.

Rnd 2: Sc 20.

Rnd 3: (Sc 3, sc2tog) 4 times—16 sts.

Rnd 3: (Sc 2, sc2tog) 4 times—12 sts.

Rnds 4–5: Sc 12.

Rnd 6: (Sc 4, sc2tog) 2 times—10 sts.

Rnd 7: Sc2tog 5 times—5 sts.

Rnd 8: Sc2tog, sk 1, sc2tog—2 sts.

Fasten off yarn, close hole and weave in end.

Whipstitch the bottom edge of the fin to the top of the body, with the front corner of the fin lining up with Rnd 13 of the body.

Tail

With A, loosely ch 12.

Rnd 1: Working in back ridge loops, sc 10, sc 3 in next st. Rotate chain so front loops of chain are facing up. Starting in next st, sc 9, sc 2 in next st—24 sts.

Rnd 2: Sc 2 in next st, sc 9, sc 2 in next 3 sts, sc 9, sc 2 in next 2 sts—30 sts.

Rnds 3–4: Sc 30.

Stuff tail. Flatten open edge to line up stitches. Working through both edges at the same time, sc to end of row to close the seam.

With A yarn on tapestry needle, attach the yarn in the middle of Rnd 1 at the base of the tail. Working from front to back, loop yarn over the top of the tail and back to starting point at the tail base. Repeat 1–2 more times, pulling tightly to cinch down the middle of the tail to create the two sides of the fin. Fasten off yarn to secure.

Whipstitch the bottom edge of the tail to the back of the body.

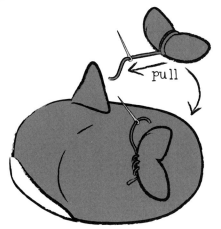

Side Fins (make 2)

With A, make a 6-st AR.

Rnd 1: Sc 1, sc 2 in next st, hdc 2 in next 2 sts, sc 2 in next st, (sc 1, ch 2, sc 1) in next st—10 sts.

Fasten off, leaving a long tail for sewing.

With A, whipstitch the rounded sides of the fins to the sides of the body just above the top edge of the belly, 8 rnds behind the eyes.

FINISHING: Double a long piece of the bulky black yarn on a tapestry needle and embroider an eyebrow over each eye. Embroider two short stitches to the front of the face above the top edge of the white belly for nostrils. Embroider three sets of long stitches on either side of the body between the eye and the side fins for gills. Embroider a zigzag pattern of short stitches to the front of the belly for teeth.

Weave in any remaining yarn tails.

Ulani Unicorn

Is there anything more magical than going on a fantastic dreamland adventure with Ulani Unicorn? No, there is not!

YARNS

Super Bulky Bernat® Blanket™ Yarn—
(A) #04005 White (200yds/185m)
(B) #12003 School Bus Yellow
(50yds/45m)
(C) #12013 Sweet & Sour Variegated
(50yds/45m)

Bulky Berroco® Comfort®
Chunky—#5734 Liquorice

Optional (for child-safe eyes):
Worsted Berroco® Comfort®—#9734
Liquorice. See page 13 for pattern.

NOTIONS

• Size M/N (9.0mm) crochet hook
• Two 21mm black safety eyes
• Large steel tapestry needle
• Scissors
• Polyester fiberfill (12oz/340g)
• *Optional:* Large safety pins for place markers, bamboo straight pins

FINISHED SIZE

13" long, 9" wide, 7" tall

Ulani Unicorn

Body

With A, loosely ch 8.

Rnd 1: Working in back ridge loops, sc 6, sc 3 in next st. Rotate chain so front loops of chain are facing up. Starting in next st, sc 5, sc 2 in next st—16 sts.

Rnd 2: Sc 2 in next st, sc 5, sc 2 in next 3 sts, sc 5, sc 2 in next 2 sts—22 sts.

Rnd 3: Sc 2 in next st, sc 7, sc 2 in next 4 sts, sc 7, sc 2 in next 3 sts—30 sts.

Rnd 4: Sc 2 in next 2 sts, sc 9, sc 2 in next 6 sts, sc 9, sc 2 in next 4 sts—42 sts.

Rnd 5: (Sc 3, sc 2 in next st, sc 3) 6 times—48 sts.

Rnd 6: (Sc 2, sc 2 in next st) 16 times—64 sts.

Rnds 7–8: Sc 64.

Rnd 9: (Sc 2, sc2tog) 16 times—48 sts.

Rnds 10–27: Sc 48.

Rnd 28: (Sc 2, sc2tog, sc 2) 8 times—40 sts.

Rnd 29: (Sc 3, sc2tog) 8 times—32 sts.

Rnd 30: (Sc 1, sc2tog, sc 1) 8 times—24 sts.

Rnd 31: (Sc 1, sc2tog) 8 times—16 sts.

Fasten off, leaving a long tail for sewing. Stuff body firmly, but do not close hole.

If using plastic safety eyes, attach eyes to the front of the body between Rnds 3 and 4. You may wish to remove a bit of stuffing after positioning the eyes to make installing the eye backings easier. For children under 3, sew on crocheted eyes (page 13) or embroider eyes using the bulky black yarn and a tight grouping of satin stitches (page 10).

Using a mattress stitch, bring the edges of the hole in the back of the body together and sew the seam closed in a straight line level with the ch-8 at the beginning of your work.

Ears (make 2)

With A, loosely ch 4.

Row 1: Starting in 2nd ch from hook, sc 3 and turn—3 sts.

Row 2: Ch 1, sc 1, sk 1, sc 1 and turn—2 sts.

Row 3: Ch 1, sc2tog and pm—1 st.

Continue to sc evenly along the side, bottom edge, and opposite side of the ear or tail until you reach the marker. (Sc 1, ch 2, sl st 1) in marked st, fasten off in next st and cut yarn, leaving a long tail for sewing.

With A, whipstitch the rounded base of the ears to the head about 4–5 rnds behind the eyes.

Muzzle

With A, loosely ch 8.

Rnd 1: Working in back ridge loops, sc 6, sc 3 in next st. Rotate chain so front loops of chain are facing up. Starting in next st, sc 5, sc 2 in next st—16 sts.

Rnd 2: Sc 2 in next st, sc 5, sc 2 in next 3 sts, sc 5, sc 2 in next 2 sts—22 sts.

Rnd 3: Sc 2 in next st, sc 7, sc 2 in next 4 sts, sc 7, sc 2 in next 3 sts—30 sts.

Rnds 4–5: Sc 30.

Fasten off, leaving a long tail for sewing.

Line up the top edge of the muzzle between the eyes and the bottom edge of the muzzle across the lower edge of the face (around Rnd 5). Sew open edge down with mattress stitch, stuffing muzzle firmly before closing seam.

Nostrils (make 2)

With A, make a 5-st AR but do not join. Cut yarn and pull through current st to fasten off.

Pinch the 1st and 5th sts of the 5-st AR together and secure with a couple of stitches. With the pinched corners pointed toward each other, sew the nostrils to the middle of the muzzle with about 6–7 stitches between them.

Horn

With B, make an 8-st AR.

Rnd 1: In bl, sc 8.

Rnd 2: In bl, sc2tog, sc 6—7 sts.

Rnd 3: In bl, sc2tog, sc 5—6 sts.

Rnd 4: In bl, sc2tog, sc 4—5 sts.

Stuff horn.

Rnd 5: In bl, sc2tog, sc 3—4 sts.

Rnd 6: In bl, sk 1, sl st 1 in next st and fasten off.

Cut yarn and fasten off, leaving a long tail for sewing.

Stuff horn lightly. Mattress stitch open edge of horn to top of head between the ears.

Big Curls (make 6)

With C, loosely ch 15.

Starting in 2nd ch from hook, hdc 3 in each st to end.

Small Curls (make 6)

With C, loosely ch 10.

Starting in 2nd ch from hook, sc 3 in each st to end.

Arrange a mix of 9 curls between the ears and horn until you are happy with the placement. Whipstitch the ends of the curls to the head.

Group the remaining 3 curls at the back of the body to form the base of the tail, keeping the ends of the curls close together when you attach them using C and a whipstitch.

Legs (make 4)

Starting with B, make a 6-st AR.

Rnd 1: Sc 2 in each st around—12 sts.

Cut B, change to A.

Rnd 2: In bl, sc2tog 6 times—6 sts.

Rnd 3: Sc 6.

Fasten off, leaving a long tail for sewing.

Stuff and mattress stitch the open edges of the legs to the bottom of the body (around Rnds 12–13 for the front legs and Rnds 22–23 for the back legs) with about 8 sts of space between the inside edges of the legs.

NOTE: When sewing the legs to the bottom of the body, leave the yarn tails unsecured until all 4 legs are sewn in place to allow for easier removal and adjustments. Once you are satisfied with the leg placement, fasten off the yarn tails and weave in the ends.

FINISHING: Double a long piece of the bulky black yarn on a tapestry needle and embroider an eyebrow over each eye.

Weave in any remaining yarn tails.

Draco Dragon

Darling Draco Dragon is all decked out with wings, frills, claws, and teeth. The only thing missing is a few puffs of crocheted smoke!

YARNS

Super Bulky Bernat® Blanket™ Yarn—
(A) #13001 Race Car Red (250yds/228m)
(B) #12003 School Bus Yellow
   (150yds/137m)

(C) #04005 White (10yds/8m)

Bulky Berroco® Comfort®
Chunky—#5734 Liquorice (2yds/2m)

Optional (for child-safe eyes):
Worsted Berroco® Comfort®—#9734
Liquorice. See page 13 for pattern.

NOTIONS

- Size M/N (9.0mm) crochet hook
- Two 21mm black safety eyes
- Large steel tapestry needle
- Scissors
- Polyester fiberfill (12oz/340g)
- *Optional*: Large safety pins for place
  markers, bamboo straight pins

FINISHED SIZE

16" long, 9" wide, 7" tall

Draco Dragon

Body

With A, loosely ch 8.

Rnd 1: Working in back ridge loops, sc 6, sc 3 in next st. Rotate chain so front loops of chain are facing up. Starting in next st, sc 5, sc 2 in next st—16 sts.

Rnd 2: Sc 2 in next st, sc 5, sc 2 in next 3 sts, sc 5, sc 2 in next 2 sts—22 sts.

Rnd 3: Sc 2 in next st, sc 7, sc 2 in next 4 sts, sc 7, sc 2 in next 3 sts—30 sts.

Rnd 4: Sc 2 in next 2 sts, sc 9, sc 2 in next 6 sts, sc 9, sc 2 in next 4 sts—42 sts.

Rnd 5: (Sc 3, sc 2 in next st, sc 3) 6 times—48 sts.

Rnd 6: (Sc 2, sc 2 in next st) 16 times—64 sts.

Rnds 7–8: Sc 64.

Rnd 9: (Sc 2, sc2tog) 16 times—48 sts.

Rnds 10–27: Sc 48.

Rnd 28: (Sc 2, sc2tog, sc 2) 8 times—40 sts.

Rnd 29: (Sc 3, sc2tog) 8 times—32 sts.

Rnd 30: (Sc 1, sc2tog, sc 1) 8 times—24 sts.

Rnd 31: (Sc 1, sc2tog) 8 times—16 sts.

Fasten off, leaving a long tail for sewing. Stuff body firmly, but do not close hole.

If using plastic safety eyes, attach eyes to the front of the body between Rnds 3 and 4. You may wish to remove a bit of stuffing after positioning the eyes to make installing the eye backings easier. For children under 3, sew on crocheted eyes (page 13) or embroider eyes using the bulky black yarn and a tight grouping of satin stitches (page 10).

Using a mattress stitch, bring the edges of the hole in the back of the body together and sew the seam closed in a straight line level with the ch-8 at the beginning of your work.

With A, draw a long stitch out from the middle of the ch-8 in the center of the face and into the bottom of the head (around Rnd 6) before drawing the yarn out through the starting point in the center of the face again. Repeat 2–3 times, pulling tightly to shape the cheeks.

Snout

With A, loosely ch 11.

Rnd 1: Working in back ridge loops, sc 9, sc 3 in next st. Rotate chain so front loops of chain are facing up. Starting in next st, sc 8, sc 2 in next st—22 sts.

Rnd 2: Sc 2 in next st, sc 7, sc 2 in next 4 sts, sc 7, sc 2 in next 3 sts—30 sts.

Rnd 3: Sc 2 in next 2 sts, sc 9, sc 2 in next 6 sts, sc 9, sc 2 in next 4 sts—42 sts.

Rnd 4: Sc 42.

Rnd 5: (Sc 5, sc2tog) 6 times—36 sts.

Rnd 6: (Sc 4, sc2tog) 6 times—30 sts.

Rnd 7: (Sc 1, sc2tog) 10 times—20 sts.

Fasten off, leaving a long tail for sewing.

Line up the top edge of the snout between the eyes and the bottom edge of the snout across the lower edge of the face (around Rnd 5). Sew open edge down with mattress stitch, stuffing snout firmly before closing seam.

With A, draw a long stitch out from the front of the snout and into the bottom back edge of the snout before drawing the yarn out through the starting point in the center of the snout again. Repeat 2–3 times, pulling tightly to shape the snout.

Nostrils (make 2)

With A, make a 5-st AR but do not join. Turn and work semicircle shape in rows.

Row 1: Ch 1, sl st 5 and fasten off, leaving a long tail for sewing.

Pinch the corners of nostril together and secure with a couple of stitches. Sew the pinched corner of the nostril to the upper half of the snout 2–3 rnds in front of the eyes.

Teeth (make 2)

With C, make a 3-st AR.

Rnd 1: Sc 2 in each st around and fasten off—6 sts.

Fasten off, leaving a long tail for sewing.

Mattress stitch the open edges of the teeth to the bottom of the snout.

Ears (make 2)

With A, loosely ch 4.

Row 1: Starting in 2nd ch from hook, sc 3 and turn—3 sts.

Row 2: Ch 1, sc 1, sk 1, sc 1 and turn—2 sts.

Row 3: Ch 1, sc 2 and turn.

Row 4: Ch 1, sc2tog and pm—1 st.

Continue to sc evenly along the side, bottom edge, and opposite side of the ear until you reach the marker. (Sc 1, ch 2, sl st 1) in marked st, fasten off in next st and cut yarn, leaving a long tail for sewing.

Whipstitch the rounded base of the ears to the head about 4-5 rnds behind the eyes.

Wings (make 2)

With A, make an 8-st AR but do not join. Turn and work semicircle shape in rows.

Row 1: Ch 1, sl st 2, sc 2 in next 4 sts, sl st 2 and turn—12 sts.

Row 2: Ch 1, sl st 2, [(sl st 1, ch 3, sl st 1) in next st, sl st 1] 4 times, sl st 2.

Fasten off, leaving a long tail for sewing.

Pinch the corners of the wing's flat edge together and secure with a couple of stitches. Sew the pinched corner of the wings to the sides of the body with a few whipstitches, 5 rnds behind the ears.

Tail

With A, make a 4-st AR.

Rnd 1: (Sc 1, sc 2 in next st) 2 times—6 sts.

Rnd 2: (Sc 1, sc 2 in next st, sc 1) 2 times—8 sts.

Rnd 3: Sc 8.

Rnd 4: (Sc 3, sc 2 in next st) 2 times—10 sts.

Rnd 5: Sc 10.

Rnd 6: (Sc 4, sc 2 in next st) 2 times—12 sts.

Rnd 7: (Sc 2, sc 2 in next st, sc 3) 2 times—14 sts.

Rnd 8: (Sc 6, sc 2 in next st) 2 times—16 sts.

Fasten off, leaving a long tail for sewing.

Sew open edge of tail to back of body, stuffing before closing seam.

Cheek & Tail Frill (make 2 in A and 1 in B)

With A or B, make a 6-st AR.

Rnd 1: (Sc 1, ch 5. Starting in 2nd ch from hook and working in back ridge loops, sl st 4, sl st in st at base of ch-5) 3 times, sl st 3 and fasten off.

Whipstitch the rounded edge of "A" frills to sides of face 5–6 rnds behind the eyes. Whipstitch rounded edge of "B" frill to end of tail.

Belly

In B, loosely ch 8.

Rnd 1: Working in back ridge loops, sc 6, sc 3 in next st. Rotate chain so front loops of chain are facing up. Starting in next st, sc 5, sc 2 in next st—16 sts.

Rnd 2: Sc 2 in next st, sc 5, sc 2 in next 3 sts, sc 5, sc 2 in next 2 sts—22 sts.

Rnd 3: Sc 2 in next st, sc 7, sc 2 in next 4 sts, sc 7, sc 2 in next 3 sts—30 sts.

Rnd 4: Sc 2 in next 2 sts, sc 9, sc 2 in next 6 sts, sc 9, sc 2 in next 4 sts—42 sts.

Rnd 5: (Sc 3, sc 2 in next st, sc 3) 6 times—48 sts.

Rnd 6: (Sc 2, sc 2 in next st) 16 times—64 sts.

Fasten off, leaving a long tail for sewing.

Using a backstitch, sew the edge of the belly to the bottom of the body.

Back Ridge

In B, loosely ch 25.

Row 1: Starting in 2nd ch from hook and working in back ridge loops, (sl st 1, sc 1, ch 4, sc 1 in base stitch of ch-4, sl st 1) 8 times.

Starting along the top edge of the tail, whipstitch the chained edge of the back ridge to the top of the tail and back.

Legs & Feet (make 4)

Starting with A, make a 6 st AR.

Rnd 1: Sc 2 in each st around—12 sts.

Rnd 2: In fl, sc 4 and turn. Cut A and change to B. Ch 1, working in the bl of these 4 sts only, (sl st 1, ch 2, sl st 1) in bl of next 3 sts, (sl st 1, ch 2, cut B, change to A, sl st 1) in bl of 4th st. Turn. Working directly behind the toes and claws in the bls of Rnd 1 sts, sc 12—12 sts.

Rnd 3: Sc2tog 6 times—6 sts.

Fasten off, leaving a long tail for sewing.

Stuff and mattress stitch the open edges of the legs to the bottom of the body (around Rnds 12–13 for the front legs and Rnds 22–23 for the back legs) with about 8 sts of space between the inside edges of the legs. The legs may overlap the belly slightly.

NOTE: When sewing the legs to the bottom of the body, leave the yarn tails unsecured until all 4 legs are sewn in place to allow for easier removal and adjustments. Once you are satisfied with the leg placement, fasten off the yarn tails and weave in the ends.

FINISHING: Double a long piece of the bulky black yarn on a tapestry needle and embroider an eyebrow over each eye.

Weave in any remaining yarn tails.

Bella Bumblebee

Buzz Buzz Buzz! Sweet-as-honey Bella Bumblebee is sure to buzz her way right into your heart!

YARNS

Super Bulky Bernat® Blanket™ Yarn—
(A) #10040 Coal (180yds/165m)
(B) #12003 School Bus Yellow
    (75yds/68m)
(C) #04005 White (10yds/9m)

Optional (for embroidered eyes):
Bulky Berroco® Comfort®
Chunky—#5734 Liquorice (2yds/2m)

Optional (for child-safe eyes):
Worsted Berroco® Comfort®—#9734
Liquorice. See page 13 for pattern.

NOTIONS

- Size M/N (9.0mm) crochet hook
- Two 21mm black safety eyes
- Large steel tapestry needle
- Scissors
- Polyester fiberfill (12oz/340g)
- *Optional:* Large safety pins for place markers, bamboo straight pins

FINISHED SIZE

13" long, 9" wide, 7" tall

Bella Bumblebee

Body

With A, loosely ch 8.

Rnd 1: Working in back ridge loops, sc 6, sc 3 in next st. Rotate chain so front loops of chain are facing up. Starting in next st, sc 5, sc 2 in next st—16 sts.

Rnd 2: Sc 2 in next st, sc 5, sc 2 in next 3 sts, sc 5, sc 2 in next 2 sts—22 sts.

Rnd 3: Sc 2 in next st, sc 7, sc 2 in next 4 sts, sc 7, sc 2 in next 3 sts—30 sts.

Rnd 4: Sc 2 in next 2 sts, sc 9, sc 2 in next 6 sts, sc 9, sc 2 in next 4 sts—42 sts.

Rnd 5: (Sc 3, sc 2 in next st, sc 3) 6 times—48 sts.

Rnd 6: (Sc 2, sc 2 in next st) 16 times—64 sts.

Rnds 7–8: Sc 64.

Rnd 9: (Sc 2, sc2tog) 16 times—48 sts.

Refer to Jogless Color Changes on page 7 for tips on how to create smoother stripe transitions from one round to the next!

Rnds 10–27: Starting with B, alt 2 rnds in B and 2 rnds in A, ending with 2 rnds of B. Cut B.

Continue in A.

Rnd 28: (Sc 2, sc2tog, sc 2) 8 times—40 sts.

Rnd 29: (Sc 3, sc2tog) 8 times—32 sts.

Rnd 30: (Sc 1, sc2tog, sc 1) 8 times—24 sts.

Rnd 31: (Sc 1, sc2tog) 8 times—16 sts.

Fasten off, leaving a long tail for sewing. Stuff body firmly, but do not close hole.

If using plastic safety eyes, attach eyes to the front of the body between Rnds 3 and 4. You may wish to remove a bit of stuffing after positioning the eyes to make installing the eye backings easier. For children under 3, sew on crocheted eyes (page 13) or embroider eyes using the bulky black yarn and a tight grouping of satin stitches (page 10).

Using a mattress stitch, bring the edges of the hole in the back of the body together and sew the seam closed in a straight line level with the ch-8 at the beginning of your work.

Antenna (make 2)

With A, loosely ch 4.

Row 1: Starting in 2nd ch from hook, sc 3 and turn—3 sts.

Row 2: Ch 1, sc 1, sk 1, sc 1 and turn—2 sts.

Row 3: Ch 1, sc2tog and turn—1 st.

Row 4: Ch 1, sc 1 and turn—1 st.

Row 5: Ch 1, sc 1—1 st.

Continue to sc evenly along the side, base, and opposite side of the antenna, fastening off in the 1st and only st of Row 5. Cut and fasten off yarn, leaving a long tail for sewing.

Fold the long edges of Rows 5 through 3 together and whipstitch these edges closed. Leave the edges of Rows 2 and 1 open to create the rounded top end of the antenna stalk.

Whipstitch the bottom of the antenna stalk to the head 4–5 rnds behind the eyes.

Wings (make 2)

With C, make an 8-st AR but do not join. Turn and work semicircle shape in rows.

Row 1: Ch 1, sc 2 in each st—16 sts.

Fasten off, leaving a long tail for sewing.

Pinch corners of wing shape together and secure with a few stitches. With C, whipstitch the pinched end of the wings to the back of the bee between stripes 3 and 4.

Stinger

With C, make a 3-st AR.

Rnd 1: Sc 2 in next st, sc 1, sc 2 in next st—5 sts.

Rnd 2: Sc 5.

Fasten off yarn.

Stuff and mattress stitch the open edge of the stinger to the back of the body.

Legs (make 6)

In A, make a 6-st AR.

Rnd 1: Sc 2 in each st around—12 sts.

Rnd 2: Sc2tog 6 times—6 sts.

Fasten off, leaving a long tail for sewing.

Stuff and mattress stitch the open edges of the legs to the bottom of the body (around Rnds 11–12, 17–18, and 23–24) with about 8 sts of space between the inside edges of the legs.

NOTE: When sewing the legs to the bottom of the body, leave the yarn tails unsecured until all 6 legs are sewn in place to allow for easier removal and adjustments. Once you are satisfied with the leg placement, fasten off the yarn tails and weave in the ends.

FINISHING: Weave in any remaining yarn tails.

Lily Lovebug

Lily Lovebug wears her heart on her sleeve (or shell)
as the case may be!

YARNS

Super Bulky Bernat® Blanket™ Yarn—
(A) #10040 Coal (180yds/165m)
(B) #12008 Pixie Pink (100yds/91m)

Optional (for embroidered eyes):
Bulky Berroco® Comfort®
Chunky—#5734 Liquorice

Optional (for child-safe eyes):
Worsted Berroco® Comfort®—#9734
Liquorice. See page 13 for pattern.

NOTIONS

- Size M/N (9.0mm) crochet hook
- Two 21mm black safety eyes
- Large steel tapestry needle
- Scissors
- Polyester fiberfill (12oz/340g)
- *Optional*: Large safety pins for place markers, bamboo straight pins

FINISHED SIZE

13" long, 9" wide, 7" tall

Lily Lovebug

Body

With A, loosely ch 8.

Rnd 1: Working in back ridge loops, sc 6, sc 3 in next st. Rotate chain so front loops of chain are facing up. Starting in next st, sc 5, sc 2 in next st—16 sts.

Rnd 2: Sc 2 in next st, sc 5, sc 2 in next 3 sts, sc 5, sc 2 in next 2 sts—22 sts.

Rnd 3: Sc 2 in next st, sc 7, sc 2 in next 4 sts, sc 7, sc 2 in next 3 sts—30 sts.

Rnd 4: Sc 2 in next 2 sts, sc 9, sc 2 in next 6 sts, sc 9, sc 2 in next 4 sts—42 sts.

Rnd 5: (Sc 3, sc 2 in next st, sc 3) 6 times—48 sts.

Rnd 6: (Sc 2, sc 2 in next st) 16 times—64 sts.

Rnds 7–8: Sc 64.

Rnd 9: (Sc 2, sc2tog) 16 times—48 sts.

Rnds 10–27: Sc 48.

Rnd 28: (Sc 2, sc2tog, sc 2) 8 times—40 sts.

Rnd 29: (Sc 3, sc2tog) 8 times—32 sts.

Rnd 30: (Sc 1, sc2tog, sc 1) 8 times—24 sts.

Rnd 31: (Sc 1, sc2tog) 8 times—16 sts.

Fasten off, leaving a long tail for sewing. Stuff body firmly, but do not close hole.

If using plastic safety eyes, attach eyes to the front of the body between Rnds 3 and 4. You may wish to remove a bit of stuffing after positioning the eyes to make installing the eye backings easier. For children under 3, sew on crocheted eyes (page 13) or embroider eyes using the bulky black yarn and a tight grouping of satin stitches (page 10).

Using a mattress stitch, bring the edges of the hole in the back of the body together and sew the seam closed in a straight line level with the ch-8 at the beginning of your work.

Shell (make 2)

With B, ch 25 and turn.

Row 1: Starting in 2nd ch from hook, sc 23, sc 2 in next st and turn—25 sts.

Row 2: Ch 1, sc 25 and turn.

Row 3: Ch 1, sc 24, sc 2 in next st and turn—26 sts.

Row 4: Ch 1, sc 26 and turn.

Row 5: Ch 1, sc 25, sc 2 in next st and turn—27 sts.

Row 6: Ch 1, sc 27 and turn.

Row 7: Ch 1, sc 26, sc 2 in next st and turn—28 sts.

Row 8: Ch 1, sc 28 and turn.

Row 9: Ch 1, sc 27, sc 2 in next st and turn—29 sts.

Rows 10–13: Ch 1, sc 29 and turn.

Row 14: Ch 1, sc 29. Do not turn.

Sc around entire edge of work until you reach your starting point and fasten off.

Sew the flat edges of the shell halves to the top of the body between Rnds 7 and 8. Overlap the shell's curved ends in the back of the body and pin in place. There will be a small space that will form between the inside edges of the two shell halves. Use a backstitch and B to sew the edges of the shells down.

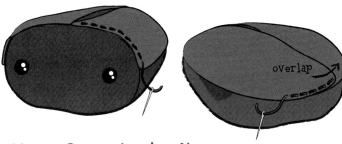

Heart Spots (make 6)

With A, make a 7-st AR but do not join. Turn and work semicircle shape in rows.

Row 1: Ch 1, hdc 2 in next st, sc 1, sl st 1, (sl st 1, ch 1, sl st 1) in next st, sl st 1, sc 1, hdc 2 in next st—10 sts.

Pull yarn through current loop to fasten off. Cut yarn, leaving a long tail for sewing. Pin hearts to shell. With A, backstitch along the edges to sew heart spots to back of shell.

Antenna (make 2)

With A, loosely ch 4,

Row 1: Starting in 2nd ch from hook, sc 3 and turn—3 sts.

Row 2: Ch 1, sc 1, sk 1, sc 1 and turn—2 sts.

Row 3: Ch 1, sc2tog and turn—1 st.

Row 4: Ch 1, sc 1 and turn—1 st.

Row 5: Ch 1, sc 1—1 st.

Continue to sc evenly along the side, base, and opposite side of the antenna, fastening off in the 1st and only st of Row 5. Cut and fasten off yarn, leaving a long tail for sewing.

Fold the long edges of Rows 5 through 3 together and whipstitch these edges closed. Leave the edges of Rows 2 and 1 open to create the rounded top end of the antenna stalk.

Whipstitch the bottom of the antenna stalk to the head 3 rnds behind the eyes, directly in front of the shell's front edge.

Legs (make 6)

In A, make a 6-st AR.

Rnd 1: Sc 2 in each st around—12 sts.

Rnd 2: Sc2tog 6 times—6 sts.

Fasten off, leaving a long tail for sewing.

Stuff and mattress stitch the open edges of the legs to the bottom of the body (around Rnds 11–12, 17–18, and 23–24) with about 8 sts of space between the inside edges of the legs.

NOTE: When sewing the legs to the bottom of the body, leave the yarn tails unsecured until all 6 legs are sewn in place to allow for easier removal and adjustments. Once you are satisfied with the leg placement, fasten off the yarn tails and weave in the ends.

FINISHING: Weave in any remaining yarn tails.

Bonnie Butterfly

Bonnie Butterfly won't be fluttering off the ground anytime soon, but that's okay. She's happy to sit on your lap and smell the flowers.

YARNS

Super Bulky Bernat® Blanket™ Yarn—
(A) #10040 Coal (180yds/165m)
(B) #04734 Baby Teal (5yds/4m)
(C) #04310 Baby Lilac (5yds/4m)
(D) #04005 White (5yds/4m)

Optional (for embroidered eyes):
Bulky Berroco® Comfort®—#5734
Liquorice (2yds/2m)

Optional (for child-safe eyes): Worsted
Berroco® Comfort®—#9734 Liquorice.
See page 13 for pattern.

NOTIONS

- Size M/N (9.0mm) crochet hook
- Two 21mm black safety eyes
- Large steel tapestry needle
- Scissors
- Polyester fiberfill (12oz/340g)
- *Optional*: Large safety pins for place markers, bamboo straight pins

FINISHED SIZE

13" long, 9" wide, 7" tall

Bonnie Butterfly

Body

With A, loosely ch 8.

Rnd 1: Working in back ridge loops, sc 6, sc 3 in next st. Rotate chain so front loops of chain are facing up. Starting in next st, sc 5, sc 2 in next st—16 sts.

Rnd 2: Sc 2 in next st, sc 5, sc 2 in next 3 sts, sc 5, sc 2 in next 2 sts—22 sts.

Rnd 3: Sc 2 in next st, sc 7, sc 2 in next 4 sts, sc 7, sc 2 in next 3 sts—30 sts.

Rnd 4: Sc 2 in next 2 sts, sc 9, sc 2 in next 6 sts, sc 9, sc 2 in next 4 sts—42 sts.

Rnd 5: (Sc 3, sc 2 in next st, sc 3) 6 times—48 sts.

Rnd 6: (Sc 2, sc 2 in next st) 16 times—64 sts.

Rnds 7–8: Sc 64.

Rnd 9: (Sc 2, sc2tog) 16 times—48 sts.

Rnds 10–27: Sc 48.

Rnd 28: (Sc 2, sc2tog, sc 2) 8 times—40 sts.

Rnd 29: (Sc 3, sc2tog) 8 times—32 sts.

Rnd 30: (Sc 1, sc2tog, sc 1) 8 times—24 sts.

Rnd 31: (Sc 1, sc2tog) 8 times—16 sts.

Fasten off, leaving a long tail for sewing. Stuff body firmly, but do not close hole.

If using plastic safety eyes, attach eyes to the front of the body between Rnds 3 and 4. You may wish to remove a bit of stuffing after positioning the eyes to make installing the eye backings easier. For children under 3, sew on crocheted eyes (page 13) or embroider eyes using the bulky black yarn and a tight grouping of satin stitches (page 10).

Using a mattress stitch, bring the edges of the hole in the back of the body together and sew the seam closed in a straight line level with the ch-8 at the beginning of your work.

Antenna (make 2)

With A, loosely ch 4,

Row 1: Starting in 2nd ch from hook, sc 3 and turn—3 sts.

Row 2: Ch 1, sc 1, sk 1, sc 1 and turn—2 sts.

Row 3: Ch 1, sc2tog and turn—1 st.

Row 4: Ch 1, sc 1 and turn—1 st.

Row 5: Ch 1, sc 1—1 st.

Continue to sc evenly along the side, base, and opposite side of the antenna, fastening off in the 1st and only st of Row 5. Cut and fasten off yarn, leaving a long tail for sewing.

Fold the long edges of Rows 5 through 3 together and whipstitch these edges closed. Leave the edges of Rows 2 and 1 open to create the rounded top end of the antenna stalk.

Whipstitch the bottom of the antenna stalk to the head 3 rnds behind the eyes.

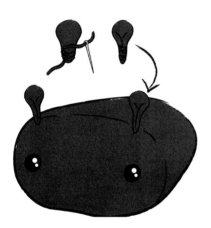

Wings (make 2)

Starting with B, make a 7-st AR but do not join. Cut B, change to D, ch 1 and turn to work semicircle shape in rows.

Row 1: (Hdc 1, pm, hdc 2) in next st, sc 2, sc 2 in next st, sc 2, hdc 3 in next st and turn—12 sts.

Cut D, change to C.

Row 2: Ch 1, sc 2 in next 3 sts, sc 2, sc 3 in next 2 sts, sc 2, sc 2 in next 3 sts and pm.

Continue to sc along remaining edge of C until you reach the marked st and fasten off.

Sew flat edges of wings to back of body.

Legs (make 6)

In A, make a 6 st AR.

Rnd 1: Sc 2 in each st around—12 sts.

Rnd 2: Sc2tog 6 times—6 sts.

Fasten off, leaving a long tail for sewing.

Stuff and mattress stitch the open edges of the legs to the bottom of the body (around Rnds 11–12, 17–18, and 23–24) with about 8 sts of space between the inside edges of the legs.

NOTE: When sewing the legs to the bottom of the body, leave the yarn tails unsecured until all 6 legs are sewn in place to allow for easier removal and adjustments. Once you are satisfied with the leg placement, fasten off the yarn tails and weave in the ends.

FINISHING: Weave in any remaining yarn tails.

Beatrice Bunny

Floppy, lop-eared Beatrice Bunny makes a great springtime gift if you can bear to part with this carrot-eating cutie.

YARNS

Super Bulky Bernat® Blanket™ Yarn—
(A) #04010 Baby Sand (200yds/180m)
(B) #04008 Vanilla (50yds/45m)

Bulky Berroco® Comfort®
Chunky—#5734 Liquorice (2yds/2m)

Optional (for child-safe eyes and nose):
Worsted Berroco® Comfort®—#9734
Liquorice and #9723 Rosebud.
See page 13 for patterns.

NOTIONS

- Size M/N (9.0mm) crochet hook
- Two 21mm black safety eyes and one 29mm pink heart safety nose
- Large steel tapestry needle
- Scissors
- Polyester fiberfill (12oz/340g)
- *Optional*: Large safety pins for place markers, bamboo straight pins

FINISHED SIZE

13" long, 9" wide, 7" tall

Beatrice Bunny

Body

With A, loosely ch 8.

Rnd 1: Working in back ridge loops, sc 6, sc 3 in next st. Rotate chain so front loops of chain are facing up. Starting in next st, sc 5, sc 2 in next st—16 sts.

Rnd 2: Sc 2 in next st, sc 5, sc 2 in next 3 sts, sc 5, sc 2 in next 2 sts—22 sts.

Rnd 3: Sc 2 in next st, sc 7, sc 2 in next 4 sts, sc 7, sc 2 in next 3 sts—30 sts.

Rnd 4: Sc 2 in next 2 sts, sc 9, sc 2 in next 6 sts, sc 9, sc 2 in next 4 sts—42 sts.

Rnd 5: (Sc 3, sc 2 in next st, sc 3) 6 times—48 sts.

Rnd 6: (Sc 2, sc 2 in next st) 16 times—64 sts.

Rnds 7–8: Sc 64.

Rnd 9: (Sc 2, sc2tog) 16 times—48 sts.

Rnds 10–27: Sc 48.

Rnd 28: (Sc 2, sc2tog, sc 2) 8 times—40 sts.

Rnd 29: (Sc 3, sc2tog) 8 times—32 sts.

Rnd 30: (Sc 1, sc2tog, sc 1) 8 times—24 sts.

Rnd 31: (Sc 1, sc2tog) 8 times—16 sts.

Fasten off, leaving a long tail for sewing. Stuff body firmly, but do not close hole.

If using plastic safety eyes, attach eyes to the front of the body between Rnds 3 and 4. You may wish to remove a bit of stuffing after positioning the eyes to make installing the eye backings easier. For children under 3, sew on crocheted eyes (page 13) or embroider eyes using the bulky black yarn and a tight grouping of satin stitches (page 10).

Using a mattress stitch, bring the edges of the hole in the back of the body together and sew the seam closed in a straight line level with the ch-8 at the beginning of your work.

With A, draw a long stitch out from the middle of the ch-8 in the center of the face and into the bottom of the head (around Rnd 6) before drawing the yarn out through the starting point in the center of the face again. Repeat 2–3 times, pulling tightly to shape the cheeks.

Muzzle

With B, make a 7-st AR.

Rnd 1: Sc 2 in each st around—14 sts.

Rnd 2: (Sl st 3, hdc 2 in next 4 sts) 2 times—22 sts.

Fasten off, leaving a long tail for sewing.

With the hdc increases oriented on the left and right sides of the muzzle, attach safety nose between Rnds 1 and 2 directly above the center of the muzzle.

Attach open edge of muzzle to the front of the body with a mattress stitch and stuff before closing seam. For children under 3, sew on crocheted nose (page 13) or embroider nose using the bulky pink yarn and a tight grouping of satin stitches (page 10) after you have attached the muzzle to the front of the face.

To add a lip cleft below a plastic safety nose, tie the middle of an 18–20" strand of the bulky black yarn around the post of the nose. Thread your tapestry needle with the yarn tails and draw a long stitch down over the front of the muzzle, and fasten off beneath the muzzle to create the lip cleft detail.

NOTE: The same long stitch can also be embroidered onto the muzzle when using child-safe nose options (page 13).

Ears (make 2)

With A, loosely ch 5 and turn.

Row 1: Starting in 2nd ch from hook and working in back ridge loops, sc 4 and turn—4 sts.

Rows 2–8: Ch 1, sc 4 and turn—4 sts.

Row 9: Ch 1, sc 1, sc2tog, sc 1 and turn—3 sts.

Row 10: Ch 1, sc 1, sk 1, sc 1 and turn—2 sts.

Row 11: Ch 1, sc2tog and pm—1 st.

Continue to sc evenly along the side, bottom edge, and opposite side of the ear until you reach the marker. (Sc 1, ch 2, sl st 1) in marked st, fasten off in next st and cut yarn, leaving a long tail for sewing.

With A, whipstitch the rounded base of the ears to the head about 4–5 rnds behind the eyes, allowing the ears to flop over.

Belly

With B, loosely ch 8.

Rnd 1: Working in back ridge loops, sc 6, sc 3 in next st. Rotate chain so front loops of chain are facing up. Starting in next st, sc 5, sc 2 in next st—16 sts.

Rnd 2: Sc 2 in next st, sc 5, sc 2 in next 3 sts, sc 5, sc 2 in next 2 sts—22 sts.

Rnd 3: Sc 2 in next st, sc 7, sc 2 in next 4 sts, sc 7, sc 2 in next 3 sts—30 sts.

Rnd 4: Sc 2 in next 2 sts, sc 9, sc 2 in next 6 sts, sc 9, sc 2 in next 4 sts—42 sts.

Rnd 5: (Sc 3, sc 2 in next st, sc 3) 6 times—48 sts.

Rnd 6: (Sc 2, sc 2 in next st) 16 times—64 sts.

Fasten off, leaving a long tail for sewing.

Using a backstitch, sew the edge of the belly to the bottom of the body.

Back Paws (make 2)

With A, make a 6-st AR.

Rnd 1: Sc 2 in each st—12 sts.

Rnds 2–3: Sc 12.

Rnd 4: (Sc 4, sc2tog) 2 times—10 sts.

Rnd 5: (Sc 3, sc2tog) 2 times—8 sts.

Rnds 6–8: Sc 8.

Stuff foot lightly.

Rnd 9: Sc2tog 4 times.

Fasten off yarn and close hole, leaving a long tail for sewing.

Using a mattress stitch, attach the tops of the back paws to the bottom of the body (around Rnds 24–25) with the larger ends of the paws sticking out at the sides of the body.

Front Paws & Tail (make 2 in A and 1 in B)

With A or B, make a 6-st AR.

Rnd 1: Sc 2 in each st around—12 sts.

Rnd 2: Sc2tog 6 times—6 sts.

Fasten off, leaving a long tail for sewing.

Stuff and mattress stitch the open edges of the front paws to the bottom of the body (around Rnds 12–13) with about 8 sts of space between the inside edges of the paws. The front paws may overlap the belly slightly.

NOTE: When sewing the paws to the bottom of the body, leave the yarn tails unsecured until all 4 paws are sewn in place to allow for easier removal and adjustments. Once you are satisfied with the paw placement, fasten off the yarn tails and weave in the ends.

Stuff and mattress stitch the open edge of the tail to the back of the body.

FINISHING: Double a long piece of the bulky black yarn on a tapestry needle and embroider an eyebrow over each eye.

Weave in any remaining yarn tails.

Mason Mouse

Snuggly Mason Mouse would love to move into your house
(especially if you are willing to share some cheese!)

YARNS

Super Bulky Bernat® Blanket™ Yarn—
(A) #04736 Seafoam (200yds/180m)
(B) #04758 Shell Pink (50yds/45m)
(C) #04005 White (50yds/45m)

Bulky Berroco® Comfort®
Chunky—#5734 Liquorice (2yds/2m)

Optional (for child-safe eyes and nose):
Worsted Berroco® Comfort®—#9734
Liquorice. See page 13 for patterns.

NOTIONS

- Size M/N (9.0mm) crochet hook
- Two 21mm black safety eyes and one 24mm black safety eye (for nose)
- Large steel tapestry needle
- Scissors
- Polyester fiberfill (12oz/340g)
- *Optional*: Large safety pins for place markers, bamboo straight pins

FINISHED SIZE
13" long, 9" wide, 7" tall

Mason Mouse

Body

With A, loosely ch 8.

Rnd 1: Working in back ridge loops, sc 6, sc 3 in next st. Rotate chain so front loops of chain are facing up. Starting in next st, sc 5, sc 2 in next st—16 sts.

Rnd 2: Sc 2 in next st, sc 5, sc 2 in next 3 sts, sc 5, sc 2 in next 2 sts—22 sts.

Rnd 3: Sc 2 in next st, sc 7, sc 2 in next 4 sts, sc 7, sc 2 in next 3 sts—30 sts.

Rnd 4: Sc 2 in next 2 sts, sc 9, sc 2 in next 6 sts, sc 9, sc 2 in next 4 sts—42 sts.

Rnd 5: (Sc 3, sc 2 in next st, sc 3) 6 times—48 sts.

Rnd 6: (Sc 2, sc 2 in next st) 16 times—64 sts.

Rnds 7–8: Sc 64.

Rnd 9: (Sc 2, sc2tog) 16 times—48 sts.

Rnds 10–27: Sc 48.

Rnd 28: (Sc 2, sc2tog, sc 2) 8 times—40 sts.

Rnd 29: (Sc 3, sc2tog) 8 times—32 sts.

Rnd 30: (Sc 1, sc2tog, sc 1) 8 times—24 sts.

Rnd 31: (Sc 1, sc2tog) 8 times—16 sts.

Fasten off, leaving a long tail for sewing. Stuff body firmly, but do not close hole.

If using plastic safety eyes, attach eyes to the front of the body between Rnds 3 and 4. You may wish to remove a bit of stuffing after positioning the eyes to make installing the eye backings easier. For children under 3, sew on crocheted eyes (page 13) or embroider eyes using the bulky black yarn and a tight grouping of satin stitches (page 10).

Using a mattress stitch, bring the edges of the hole in the back of the body together and sew the seam closed in a straight line level with the ch-8 at the beginning of your work.

With A, draw a long stitch out from the middle of the ch-8 in the center of the face and into the bottom of the head (around Rnd 6) before drawing the yarn out through the starting point in the center of the face again. Repeat 2–3 times, pulling tightly to shape the cheeks.

Muzzle

With A, make an 8-st AR.

Rnd 1: Sc 2 in each st around—16 sts.

Rnd 2: (Sc 2, sc2tog) 4 times—12 sts.

Fasten off, leaving a long tail for sewing.

With the hdc increases oriented on the left and right sides of the muzzle, attach safety eye/nose between Rnds 1 and 2 directly above the center of the muzzle.

Attach open edge of muzzle to the front of the body with a mattress stitch and stuff before closing seam. For children under 3, sew on crocheted nose (page 13) or embroider nose using the bulky black yarn and a tight grouping of satin stitches (page 10) after you have attached the muzzle to the front of the face.

Outer Ears (make 2)

With A, make an 8-st AR.

Rnd 1: Sc 2 in each st around—16 sts.

Rnd 2: (Sc 1, sc 2 in next st) 8 times—24 sts.

Fasten off, leaving a long tail for sewing.

Inner Ears (make 2)

With B, make an 8-st AR.

Rnd 1: Sc 2 in each st around—16 sts.

Fasten off, leaving a long tail for sewing.

Sew the inner ear to the surface of the outer ear. Whipstitch the edge of the ears to the head 4–5 rnds behind the eyes.

Belly

In C, loosely ch 8.

Rnd 1: Working in back ridge loops, sc 6, sc 3 in next st. Rotate chain so front loops of chain are facing up. Starting in next st, sc 5, sc 2 in next st—16 sts.

Rnd 2: Sc 2 in next st, sc 5, sc 2 in next 3 sts, sc 5, sc 2 in next 2 sts—22 sts.

Rnd 3: Sc 2 in next st, sc 7, sc 2 in next 4 sts, sc 7, sc 2 in next 3 sts—30 sts.

Rnd 4: Sc 2 in next 2 sts, sc 9, sc 2 in next 6 sts, sc 9, sc 2 in next 4 sts—42 sts.

Rnd 5: (Sc 3, sc 2 in next st, sc 3) 6 times—48 sts.

Rnd 6: (Sc 2, sc 2 in next st) 16 times—64 sts.

Fasten off, leaving a long tail for sewing.

Using a backstitch, sew the edge of the belly to the bottom of the body.

Legs and Tail Base (make 5)

With A, make a 6-st AR.

Rnd 1: Sc 2 in each st around—12 sts.

Rnd 2: Sc2tog 6 times—6 sts.

Fasten off, leaving a long tail for sewing.

Stuff and mattress stitch the open edges of the legs to the bottom of the body (around Rnds 12–13 for the front legs and Rnds 22–23 for the back legs) with about 8 sts of space between the inside edges of the legs. The legs may overlap the belly slightly.

NOTE: When sewing the legs to the bottom of the body, leave the yarn tails unsecured until all 4 legs are sewn in place to allow for easier removal and adjustments. Once you are satisfied with the leg placement, fasten off the yarn tails and weave in the ends.

For tail base, do not stuff. Set aside.

Feet (make 4)

With B, make an 8-st AR.

Rnd 1: Sl st 2, (sl st 1, ch 3, sl st 1) in next 4 sts, sl st 2.

Fasten off, leaving a long tail for sewing.

With toes pointing toward the front of the body, mattress stitch the tops of the feet to the bottoms of the legs.

Tail

With B, make a 4-st AR.

Rnds 1–6: In bl, sc 4—4 sts.

Rnd 7: In bl, sk 1, sc 1, sk 1, sc 1.

Flatten and whipstitch the unstuffed tail base to the back of the body. Sink Rnd 1 of the tail down into the tail base and secure with a few whipstitches.

FINISHING: Double a long piece of the bulky black yarn on a tapestry needle and embroider an eyebrow over each eye.

Weave in any remaining yarn tails.

Cody Cat

Chunky Cody Cat is the perfect kitty to give lots of cuddly snuggles without leaving cat hair all over your couch.

YARNS

Super Bulky Bernat® Blanket™ Yarn—
(A) #10106 Country Blue (200yds/180m)
(B) #04008 Vanilla (75yds/68m)

Bulky Berroco® Comfort®
Chunky—#5734 Liquorice (2yds/2m)

Optional (for child-safe eyes and nose):
Worsted Berroco® Comfort®—#9734
Liquorice and #9723 Rosebud.
See page 13 for patterns.

NOTIONS

- Size M/N (9.0mm) crochet hook
- Two 21mm black safety eyes and one 29mm pink heart safety nose
- Large steel tapestry needle
- Scissors
- Polyester fiberfill (12oz/340g)
- *Optional:* Large safety pins for place markers, bamboo straight pins

FINISHED SIZE

13" long, 9" wide, 7" tall

Cody Cat

Body

With A, loosely ch 8.

Rnd 1: Working in back ridge loops, sc 6, sc 3 in next st. Rotate chain so front loops of chain are facing up. Starting in next st, sc 5, sc 2 in next st—16 sts.

Rnd 2: Sc 2 in next st, sc 5, sc 2 in next 3 sts, sc 5, sc 2 in next 2 sts—22 sts.

Rnd 3: Sc 2 in next st, sc 7, sc 2 in next 4 sts, sc 7, sc 2 in next 3 sts—30 sts.

Rnd 4: Sc 2 in next 2 sts, sc 9, sc 2 in next 6 sts, sc 9, sc 2 in next 4 sts—42 sts.

Rnd 5: (Sc 3, sc 2 in next st, sc 3) 6 times—48 sts.

Rnd 6: (Sc 2, sc 2 in next st) 16 times—64 sts.

Rnds 7–8: Sc 64.

Rnd 9: (Sc 2, sc2tog) 16 times—48 sts.

Rnds 10–27: Sc 48.

Rnd 28: (Sc 2, sc2tog, sc 2) 8 times—40 sts.

Rnd 29: (Sc 3, sc2tog) 8 times—32 sts.

Rnd 30: (Sc 1, sc2tog, sc 1) 8 times—24 sts.

Rnd 31: (Sc 1, sc2tog) 8 times—16 sts.

Fasten off, leaving a long tail for sewing. Stuff body firmly, but do not close hole.

If using plastic safety eyes, attach eyes to the front of the body between Rnds 3 and 4. You may wish to remove a bit of stuffing after positioning the eyes to make installing the eye backings easier. For children under 3, sew on crocheted eyes (page 13) or embroider eyes using the bulky black yarn and a tight grouping of satin stitches (page 10).

Using a mattress stitch, bring the edges of the hole in the back of the body together and sew the seam closed in a straight line level with the ch-8 at the beginning of your work.

With A, draw a long stitch out from the middle of the ch-8 in the center of the face and into the bottom of the head (around Rnd 6) before drawing the yarn out through the starting point in the center of the face again. Repeat 2–3 times, pulling tightly to shape the cheeks.

Muzzle

With B, make a 7-st AR.

Rnd 1: Sc 2 in each st around—14 sts.

Rnd 2: (Sl st 3, hdc 2 in next 4 sts) 2 times—22 sts.

Fasten off, leaving a long tail for sewing.

With the hdc increases oriented on the left and right sides of the muzzle, attach safety nose between Rnds 1 and 2 directly above the center of the muzzle.

Attach open edge of muzzle to the front of the body with a mattress stitch and stuff before closing seam. For children under 3, sew on crocheted nose (page 13) or embroider nose using the bulky pink yarn and a tight grouping of satin stitches (page 10) after you have attached the muzzle to the front of the face.

To add a lip cleft below a plastic safety nose, tie the middle of an 18–20″ strand of the bulky black yarn around the post of the nose. Thread your tapestry needle with the yarn tails and draw a long stitch down over the front of the muzzle, and fasten off beneath the muzzle to create the lip cleft detail.

NOTE: The same long stitch can also be embroidered onto the muzzle when using child-safe nose options (page 13).

Ears (make 2)

With A, loosely ch 4.

Row 1: Starting in 2nd ch from hook, sc 3 and turn—3 sts.

Row 2: Ch 1, sc 1, sk 1, sc 1 and turn—2 sts.

Row 3: Ch 1, sc2tog and pm—1 st.

Continue to sc evenly along the side, bottom edge, and opposite side of the ear until you reach the marker. (Sc 1, ch 2, sl st 1) in marked st, fasten off in next st and cut yarn, leaving a long tail for sewing.

Whipstitch the rounded base of the ears to the head, 4 rnds behind the eyes.

Belly

With B, loosely ch 8.

Rnd 1: Working in back ridge loops, sc 6, sc 3 in next st. Rotate chain so front loops of chain are facing up. Starting in next st, sc 5, sc 2 in next st—16 sts.

Rnd 2: Sc 2 in next st, sc 5, sc 2 in next 3 sts, sc 5, sc 2 in next 2 sts—22 sts.

Rnd 3: Sc 2 in next st, sc 7, sc 2 in next 4 sts, sc 7, sc 2 in next 3 sts—30 sts.

Rnd 4: Sc 2 in next 2 sts, sc 9, sc 2 in next 6 sts, sc 9, sc 2 in next 4 sts—42 sts.

Rnd 5: (Sc 3, sc 2 in next st, sc 3) 6 times—48 sts.

Rnd 6: (Sc 2, sc 2 in next st) 16 times—64 sts.

Fasten off, leaving a long tail for sewing.

Using a backstitch, sew the edge of the belly to the bottom of the body.

Tail

With B, make a 4-st AR.

Rnd 1: Sc 2 in each st around—8 sts.

Rnd 2: (Sc 1, sc 2 in next st) 4 times—12 sts.

Cut B, change to A.

Rnd 3: Sc 12.

Rnd 4: (Sc 4, sc2tog) 2 times—10 sts.

Rnd 5: (Sc 3, sc2tog) 2 times—8 sts.

Rnd 6: (Sc 2, sc2tog) 2 times—6 sts.

Rnds 7–8: Sc 6.

Fasten off, leaving a long tail for sewing.

Stuff tail. Using a mattress stitch, sew open edge of tail to back of body.

Legs (make 4)

Starting with B, make a 6-st AR.

Rnd 1: Sc 2 in each st around—12 sts.

Cut B, change to A.

Rnd 2: Sc2tog 6 times—6 sts.

Rnd 3: Sc 6.

Fasten off, leaving a long tail for sewing.

Stuff and mattress stitch the open edges of the legs to the bottom of the body (around Rnds 12–13 for the front legs and Rnds 22–23 for the back legs) with about 8 sts of space between the inside edges of the legs. The legs may overlap the belly slightly.

NOTE: When sewing the legs to the bottom of the body, leave the yarn tails unsecured until all 4 legs are sewn in place to allow for easier removal and adjustments. Once you are satisfied with the leg placement, fasten off the yarn tails and weave in the ends.

FINISHING: Double a long piece of the bulky black yarn on a tapestry needle and embroider an eyebrow over each eye. Embroider 2 short stitches in a sideways "V" shape, 1 rnd behind and below the eyes for a whisker detail.

Weave in any remaining yarn tails.

Danny Dog

Plump and poky Danny Dog will happily guard your home in return for hugs and his favorite treats.

YARNS

Super Bulky Bernat® Blanket™ Yarn—
(A) #10014 Sand (200yds/180m)
(B) #10029 Taupe (75yds/68m)

Bulky Berroco® Comfort®
Chunky—#5734 Liquorice (2yds/2m)

Optional (for child-safe eyes and nose):
Worsted Berroco® Comfort®—#9734
Liquorice. See page 13 for patterns.

NOTIONS

- Size M/N (9.0mm) crochet hook
- Two 21mm black safety eyes and one 29mm black triangle safety nose
- Large steel tapestry needle
- Scissors
- Polyester fiberfill (12oz/340g)
- *Optional*: Large safety pins for place markers, bamboo straight pins

FINISHED SIZE

13" long, 9" wide, 7" tall

Danny Dog

Body

With A, loosely ch 8.

Rnd 1: Working in back ridge loops, sc 6, sc 3 in next st. Rotate chain so front loops of chain are facing up. Starting in next st, sc 5, sc 2 in next st—16 sts.

Rnd 2: Sc 2 in next st, sc 5, sc 2 in next 3 sts, sc 5, sc 2 in next 2 sts—22 sts.

Rnd 3: Sc 2 in next st, sc 7, sc 2 in next 4 sts, sc 7, sc 2 in next 3 sts—30 sts.

Rnd 4: Sc 2 in next 2 sts, sc 9, sc 2 in next 6 sts, sc 9, sc 2 in next 4 sts—42 sts.

Rnd 5: (Sc 3, sc 2 in next st, sc 3) 6 times—48 sts.

Rnd 6: (Sc 2, sc 2 in next st) 16 times—64 sts.

Rnds 7–8: Sc 64.

Rnd 9: (Sc 2, sc2tog) 16 times—48 sts.

Rnds 10–27: Sc 48.

Rnd 28: (Sc 2, sc2tog, sc 2) 8 times—40 sts.

Rnd 29: (Sc 3, sc2tog) 8 times—32 sts.

Rnd 30: (Sc 1, sc2tog, sc 1) 8 times—24 sts.

Rnd 31: (Sc 1, sc2tog) 8 times—16 sts.

Fasten off, leaving a long tail for sewing. Stuff body firmly, but do not close hole.

If using plastic safety eyes, attach eyes to the front of the body between Rnds 3 and 4. You may wish to remove a bit of stuffing after positioning the eyes to make installing the eye backings easier. For children under 3, sew on crocheted eyes (page 13) or embroider eyes using the bulky black yarn and a tight grouping of satin stitches (page 10).

Using a mattress stitch, bring the edges of the hole in the back of the body together and sew the seam closed in a straight line level with the ch-8 at the beginning of your work.

With A, draw a long stitch out from the middle of the ch-8 in the center of the face and into the bottom of the head (around Rnd 6) before drawing the yarn out through the starting point in the center of the face again. Repeat 2–3 times, pulling tightly to shape the cheeks.

Muzzle

With A, make a 7-st AR.

Rnd 1: Sc 2 in each st around—14 sts.

Rnd 2: (Sc 3, hdc 2 in next 4 sts) 2 times—22 sts.

Rnds 3–4: Sc 22.

Fasten off, leaving a long tail for sewing.

With the hdc increases oriented on the left and right sides of the muzzle, attach safety nose between Rnds 1 and 2 directly above the center of the muzzle.

Attach open edge of muzzle to the front of the body with a mattress stitch and stuff before closing seam. For children under 3, sew on crocheted nose (page 13) or embroider nose using the bulky black yarn and a tight grouping of satin stitches (page 10) after you have attached the muzzle to the front of the face.

To add a lip cleft below a plastic safety nose, tie the middle of an 18–20" strand of the bulky black yarn around the post of the nose. Thread your tapestry needle with the yarn tails and draw a long stitch down over the front of the muzzle, and fasten off beneath the muzzle to create the lip cleft detail.

NOTE: The same long stitch can also be embroidered onto the muzzle when using child-safe nose options (page 13).

Ears (make 2)

With B, loosely ch 5 and turn.

Row 1: Starting in 2nd ch from hook and working in back ridge loops, sc 4 and turn—4 sts.

Row 2: Ch 1, sc 2 in next st, sc 2, sc 2 in next st and turn—6 sts.

Row 3: Ch 1, sc 6 and turn—6 sts.

Row 4: Ch 1, sc 2, sc2tog, sc 2 and turn—5 sts.

Row 5: Ch 1, sc 2, sk 1, sc 2 and turn—4 sts.

Rows 6–7: Ch 1, sc 4 and turn—4 sts.

Row 8: Ch 1, sc 1, sc2tog, sc 1 and turn—3 sts.

Rows 9–10: Ch 1, sc 3 and turn—3 sts.

Continue to sc evenly along the outer edge of the ear until you reach the other side of Row 10. Fasten off, leaving a long tail for sewing.

With B, whipstitch the rounded base of the ears to the head about 4 rnds behind the eyes, allowing the ears to flop over.

Tail

With A, make a 4-st AR.

Rnd 1: (Sc 1, sc 2 in next st) 2 times—6 sts.

Rnds 2–6: Sc 6.

Rnd 7: (Sc 2, sc 2 in next st) 2 times—8 sts.

Fasten off, leaving a long tail for sewing.

Stuff tail. Using a mattress stitch, sew open edge of tail to back of body.

Legs (make 4)

With A, make a 6-st AR.

Rnd 1: Sc 2 in each st around—12 sts.

Rnd 2: Sc2tog 6 times—6 sts.

Fasten off, leaving a long tail for sewing.

Stuff and mattress stitch the open edges of the legs to the bottom of the body (around Rnds 12–13 for the front legs and Rnds 22–23 for the back legs) with about 8 sts of space between the inside edges of the legs.

NOTE: When sewing the legs to the bottom of the body, leave the yarn tails unsecured until all 4 legs are sewn in place to allow for easier removal and adjustments. Once you are satisfied with the leg placement, fasten off the yarn tails and weave in the ends.

FINISHING: Double a long piece of the bulky black yarn on a tapestry needle and embroider an eyebrow over each eye.

Weave in any remaining yarn tails.

Bonus Critter Combinations

Couldn't find a pattern for your favorite critter in this book? Fear not! You can mix and match the pattern pieces to make something new. Grab a tail from one pattern, ears from another, and the wings from a third, and you have the makings of your very own custom critter. To get you started, here are some "critter recipe" suggestions you can make from the patterns in this book:

Narwhal

Whale Body (p. 67)
Whale Fins (p. 68)
Whale Tail (p. 68)
Unicorn Horn (p. 76)

Otter

Owl Body (p. 60)
Beaver Legs & Feet
    (p. 58)
Dragon Tail (p. 80)
Beaver Muzzle (p. 57)
Beaver Ears (p. 58)
Owl Belly (p. 62)

Raccoon

Owl Body (p. 60)—Rnds
    1–5: black, Rnd 6: white,
    Rnds 7–31: gray
Fox Cheeks and Chin
    (p. 54)
Fox Tail (p. 55)—Alternate
    black and gray stripes
Fox Ears (p. 55)
Owl Belly (p. 62)
Beaver Legs & Feet (p. 58)

Gorilla

Monkey Tail (p. 51)—
    Use for eyebrow ridge
Owl Body (p. 60)
Monkey Legs & Feet
    (p. 51)
Monkey Muzzle (p. 50)
Monkey Nostrils (p. 50)

Alligator

Dragon Legs & Feet
    (p. 81)
Dragon Body (p. 79)
Dragon Belly (p. 81)
Dragon Snout (p. 80)
Dragon Teeth (p. 80)
    —Make 6
Dragon Back Ridge
    (p. 81)—Make a longer
    27-st ch instead of 25-st ch

Hamster

Panda Body (p. 35)
Mouse Legs & Feet
    (pp. 97–98)
Mouse Muzzle (p. 97)
Mouse Inner Ears (p. 97)
Bear Tail (p. 65)

Frog

Shark Body (p. 71)
Shark Belly (p. 72)
Mouse Legs & Feet
    (pp. 97–98) —Make 2
    front legs and 4 feet
Bunny Back Paws (p. 93)—
    Back legs. Attach feet to the tapered ends of
    legs. Attach legs to side of body.
Bumblebee Antenna (p. 87)—Tongue
Eyes and Oval Nose (p. 13)—Spots

Walrus

Hippo Body (p. 32)
Hippo Muzzle (p. 33)
Hippo Nostrils (p. 33)
Cow Horns (p. 29)
Whale Tail (p. 68)
Whale Fins (p. 68)

Platypus

Beaver Body (p. 57)
Beaver Tail (p. 58)
Mouse Belly (p. 97)
Beaver Legs & Feet
(p. 58)
Duckbill (p. 19)

Zebra

Tiger Body (p. 42)
Pony Muzzle (p. 25)
Pony Nostrils (p. 25)
Pony Ears (p. 25)
Pony Legs (p. 25)
Cow Tail (p. 30)

Rhino

Hippo Body (p. 32)
Hippo Nostrils (p. 33)
Hippo Ears (p. 33)
Hippo Legs (p. 33)
Cow Tail (p. 30)
Dog Muzzle (p. 105)
Unicorn Horn (p. 76)
Cow Horn (p. 29)—
    Make only one

Koala

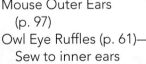

Mouse Body (p. 96)
Mouse Belly (p. 97)
Mouse Feet (p. 98)
Mouse Outer Ears
    (p. 97)
Owl Eye Ruffles (p. 61)—
    Sew to inner ears
Bear Tail (p. 65)—For nose*

*Check out the
glasseyesonline.com online store
for plastic safety koala noses*

Abbreviations & Standards

| ( ) | Work instructions within parentheses as many times as directed. |
| * | Repeat instructions following the single asterisk as directed. |

"	inch(es)
alt	alternate
beg	begin(ning)
bl(s)	back loops
ch	chain/chain stitch
fl(s)	front loops
g	gram(s)
hdc	half double crochet
m	meter(s)
mm	millimeter(s)
oz	ounce(s)
pm	place marker
rnd(s)	round(s)
RS	right side
sc	single crochet
sc2tog	single crochet 2 together
sk	skip
sl	slip
st(s)	stitch(es)
tog	together
tbl	through both loops
WS	wrong side
yd(s)	yard(s)
YO	yarn over

Yarn Weights

I-1	super fine
I-2	fine
I-3	light
I-4	medium
I-5	bulky
I-6	super bulky

Acknowledgments

Thank you to the fine folks at Dover Publications who allowed me to put this extra cuddly book together! It's been an oversized delight to design these adorable projects.

Thank you to the yarn slingers at Yarnspirations and Berroco for providing me with a beautiful array of bulky and super bulky yarns to play with and to Jerry and Carolyn from Glass Eyes Online for sneaking extra eyes and noses into my online orders!

Thank you to my agent, Amanda Luedeke, for all your encouragement and for keeping my fleeting ability to focus on whichever deadline I needed to tackle next.

And, finally, thank you to my husband, Michael, for supporting me as I crocheted into the wee hours of the night and to my children, James and Emily, for not having a pillow fight with the pattern samples.

About the Author

Megan Kreiner grew up on Long Island, New York, in a household where art was a daily part of life, and learned the crafts of knit and crochet at an early age from her grandmother, her aunt, and her mother.

A graduate with a fine arts degree in computer graphics and animation from the University of Massachusetts, Amherst, Megan is pursuing a career in the feature animation industry in Los Angeles and currently works as an animator at DreamWorks Animation.

Megan lives in California with her husband, Michael, children, James and Emily, and Olive the cat. View her work at www.mkcrochet.com.

mk crochet ®